B

READING THROUGH THE NIGHT

Reading through the Night

Jane Tompkins

University of Virginia Press

CHARLOTTESVILLE AND LONDON

University of Virginia Press
© 2018 by Jane Tompkins
All rights reserved
Printed in the United States of America on acid-free paper

First published 2018

ISBN 978-0-8139-4159-2 (cloth)
ISBN 978-0-8139-4160-8 (ebook)

9 8 7 6 5 4 3 2 1

Library of Congress Cataloging-in-Publication Data is available for this title.

Cover art: iStock / hsyncoban

To Sharon Anson
and
to the authors whose
books have kept me going
all these years

In reality, every reader is, while he is reading, the reader of his own self. The writer's work is merely a kind of optical instrument which he offers to the reader to enable him to discern what, without this book, he would perhaps never have experienced in himself.
—Marcel Proust, *In Search of Lost Time*

I wanted to describe the world because to live in an undescribed world was too lonely.
—Nicole Krauss, *The History of Love*

CONTENTS

CONTENTS

PREFACE

I had been reading all my life—as a child on summer vacations, as a student, and as a literature professor—but until I got sick and had to read for hours at a time to make the day go by, I never knew what reading could be. I read while I rested because it was all I could do. My life felt useless, my sense of self-worth was barely detectable. Then one day a stranger who subsequently became a friend gave me a book that captivated me. I couldn't get it out of my head; it was as if I'd been kidnapped. I'm an enthusiast where books are concerned, but this book—*Sir Vidia's Shadow,* Paul Theroux's account of his thirty-year friendship with V. S. Naipaul—gripped me in a way few books had ever done. There was no reason for it, since I'd had no interest in either author. I was retired, sick, and unable to work; I hadn't written anything in a long time, but I sat down at my computer and started writing, determined to find out what was going on.

The going was slow. I went down blind alleys and came up with answers that weren't the real thing. I read a lot of Naipaul, I read more Theroux, I went back to *Sir Vidia's Shadow,* probing deeper. One day, I reread a chapter where the two men have lunch in a London restaurant; it was exquisitely painful. Naipaul insults and exploits Theroux, subtly, then blatantly. Something about the way I felt when I read this scene seemed awfully familiar. Finally, it came to me. These feelings mirrored the way I felt when my husband spoke to me in a certain way, and that wasn't all. They also reflected how my mother had sometimes made me feel: ashamed, hurt, angry, and impotent. The revelation cast light in two directions. It let me see clearly for the first time a behavior pattern that had controlled my reactions to people my entire life, and it showed me that the spell *Sir Vidia's Shadow* had put me under came less from the book itself than from my own experience. That realization opened the door to a new way of reading.

Now, as I read Naipaul and Theroux, incidents from my own life began to appear; pieces of my past offered themselves unbidden. Instead of trying to analyze what the authors had written, I started to analyze the material their writing had unearthed. I began to make connections between parts of my life I'd not made before, stumbled on patterns I'd never noticed. It occurred to me that if the works of Naipaul and Theroux could have this effect, surely other books could, too. Branching out, I read what was around the house—literary criticism, journalism, contemporary novels, detective fiction—and sure enough, while the feelings these books evoked were different, the structure of the experience was the same. Just as before, by observing my reactions to what I read, I saw things about myself I didn't want to see—envy, a desire for fame, assumptions of moral superiority that were completely unfounded. Under the pressure of remembered incidents from my past, criticisms I'd started to formulate about the authors I was reading turned to dust.

From time to time, I paused to speculate on the ways reading had impacted my life—I'd started out using it as a refuge and as a vicarious form of adventure, then it metamorphosed into professional capital and a source of creativity. And now it had become a path of self-discovery. Not an easy path, but a transformative one. I went from book to book, and from memory to memory, and thus did the night of my illness yield up its treasure, bringing me face to face with who I was.

READING THROUGH THE NIGHT

Introduction

Living through Books

Not long ago, I couldn't sleep because of a book I was reading before I went to bed. It was a travel memoir by Alden Jones called *The Blind Masseuse.* It took me back to my junior year abroad in Italy. I was nineteen and wanted to get away and meet the world on my own. Jones's book brought back the taste of a peach I ate just after docking at Naples. Our group was seated in a noisy, open-air restaurant, I was sleep deprived (I'd stayed up all night talking to an enchanting man) and anxious about everything: being in a foreign country for the first time, being with people I didn't know (there was a joke going around the table that I wasn't in on)—but the peach—the peach was fat, round, beautiful, juicy, and delicious. When I bit into it the juice ran down my chin. The taste enveloped me; it let me know there was a new world here for the tasting. All I had to do was open my mouth.

The Blind Masseuse reintroduced me to the pleasures of travel as adventure, and in so doing gave me a shot of energy that took days to wear off. For many years I'd had a little-understood illness called myalgic encephalomyelitis (ME, for short), known until recently as chronic fatigue syndrome. Since fatigue, sore throats, and a low energy level had limited my ability to move around the world at will, the chance to visit exotic locales with a person whom I felt comfortable with gave me something I needed: new experiences and a lessening of loneliness. Alden Jones went to places I'd never been, and I liked her style.

Her story starts in New York, where she worked at a publishing company after graduating from college. But the thought of becoming like her boss and staring at the same view every day, year after year, stuck in her craw. So when he objected to her going out for morning coffee one day, she quit and booked a ticket for Cochabamba, Bolivia. She was my kind of girl. Jones ends up traveling around the world: Costa Rica, Nicaragua, Cuba, Cambodia, Burma, Italy, and Egypt. She leads student groups on educational trips, teaches English in Latin America, and travels on her own. If you exclude stomach trouble, nothing gut-wrenching or dramatic happens to her in any of these places, yet I read quickly and eagerly. Jones had a knack for putting me right there with her, feeling the sting and fizz of a cold Coca-Cola on a hot day, or the pangs of a bad stomachache. I needed this kind of thing: it was vicarious, but it was real. And I liked the way she reflected on what she saw.

On her first day in Bolivia, she's pelted with gravel and mango pits by three women protest marchers who laughed at her when she shouted "Why?" Later, she learned that these were Bolivian farmers demonstrating against their own government for cooperating with the U.S. Drug Enforcement Administration, whose policies had taken away their livelihood—growing coca. Jones had been standing in front of the one store in town that hadn't closed in solidarity with the march.

Jones knew nothing about any of this because she was in the habit of waiting to read about the countries she visited until after returning home. As she puts it, "I preferred to go in more or less blind, become curious about things as I observed them." Her ignorance means she has no preconceived ideas about what her experience will be like, but also no knowledge that might have kept her out of situations where people threw stones at her. In any case, the incident forces her to see that she's not the person she wishes she were—an activist who has come to Bolivia to fight injustice—but "a cerebral American, torn between a life of prestigious office jobs and the life of a vagabond who wanders into foreign lands with her eyes wide open." I devoured the book.

What appealed to me most was the experience of being young again, able to move around the world at will and feel the texture of strange things on my skin. Alden is an idealist—she wants to do good and help people—but even more she wants to see who they are, put herself in a position that allows her to sense what it's like to be them, not stand aloof judging and analyzing. She wants to plunge in and absorb things through her senses, get her hands dirty, be what Henry James called "one of the people on whom nothing is ever lost." This is the kind of person I'd wanted to be, too. Being with Alden woke me up and energized me; it made me feel that I might have enough energy to do things I hadn't done for a long time. The next thing I knew I was up and on the living room sofa writing down my reactions to the book.

It was illness that made me aware how hungry I was for the kind of experience I was getting from *The Blind Masseuse*. The spaciousness that illness created in my life, and the neediness, sensitized me to the emotions one feels as a reader but doesn't necessarily own up to, making me conscious of the way a book can pump you up or bring you down, even change your outlook on life, depending on the feelings it triggers. When I received the gift of *Sir Vidia's Shadow*, I had time, time to find out why the book had acquired such a hold on me. As I began to catch glimpses of parallels between what I was reading and my own history, I became aware of the processes that go on beneath the level of consciousness when one reads. As Diana Athill, who was Naipaul's editor, observes in her memoir *Somewhere towards the End*: "Underneath, or alongside a reader's conscious response to a text, whatever is needy in him is taking in whatever the text offers to assuage that need." By the time I came across *The Blind Masseuse,* I was able to touch down into the subterranean current of need that caused me to respond so strongly to Alden Jones's adventures. And it revealed to me that reading had played a much more important role in my life than I'd ever imagined.

If this were a piece of academic writing it might be called a phenomenology of reading, but it isn't written with reference to philosophy or literary criticism and has no claim to being a theory. I came to the works of Naipaul, Theroux, and other writers at first to see what they could tell me about these authors as human beings, and finally to answer questions which are really about myself. Sometimes I think of this book as being like the story of Theseus following Ariadne's thread through the labyrinth, or of the archaeologist Heinrich Schliemann digging for Troy. But these analogies are too high-flown. I'm more like a person with a flashlight, who has been groping around in a dusty basement or a cobwebbed attic, shining a light into obscure places and hoping to find something significant, the answer to a mystery perhaps. The insights I arrive at don't follow a plan or constitute an argument; I describe them as they present themselves, like features of a landscape emerging in the course of a long walk. This chapter sets the stage for that journey, mapping some of the discoveries I made about the role reading has played for me—as a giver and taker of energy, as a connection to another person's inner life, and as a cause of change in my own.

Energy

Among the many deprivations of illness, one of the most insidious is the loss of excitement, the highly charged, can-do feeling Jones's book gave me. I'd gotten used to feeling lethargic, blah, and without purpose—emotionally calm because there wasn't enough energy in my system to generate intensity. Her book seemed a remedy for that. It was like breathing the air of a particular place, not to be found anywhere else. I filled my lungs with it, took its essence into my body. Its effect was erotic.

The eroticism didn't come from passages about falling in love or having an affair—though Jones briefly mentions a boyfriend she had in Costa Rica and an affair with a woman she meets on her stint as a teacher for Semester at Sea—it comes from her pithy descriptions of moments and incidents that penetrated her to the core. As when she takes shelter from the rain in Cambodia with two teenage Buddhist monks with whom she manages to have a lively conversation though they share no common language, or when she describes one of her least industrious students putting his head in his hands and crying after visiting the museum that commemorates the Cambodian killing fields.

Sitting on the sofa late that night, it came to me that I'm a starving person where energy is concerned. Anything that gives me energy, even for a moment, is wonderful—the picture of a bird, a view of mountains, a joke I can really laugh at. Conversely, if I walk into a restaurant and it's noisy and chaotic, the lighting is harsh, and there are too many people, I know I'd better get out of there as soon as I can. If I don't, I'll start to feel weak and exhausted, and may have to pay for it with days of lying down.

It took me a long time to become aware of these reactions, and even longer to respect and obey them. The key in conserving energy is to listen to what your body is telling you and not pay attention to what your head is saying. This may sound easy to do, but for me it hasn't been. Ruled for so long by my mind, I tend to stay with the program—with whatever logic and planning have laid down. But when information coming in on other wavelengths says no, sticking to the plan is a bad idea. From an energetic viewpoint, illness has taught me to be careful not only about the people I'm with and the places I go, but also about the books I read. Books are just as much generators, or consumers, of energy as people and places are and can affect your system just as powerfully. They're also equally deceptive. Just as you can be fooled by a person's surface cheerfulness into believing they shouldn't be making you feel bad—why are all their smiles and good news bringing me down?—you can be fooled by the deftness and wit of someone's writing. Shapely sentences and trenchant observations that are compelling to the mind can eat away at your spirit until it flags and fails and an afternoon that started out well has sickened and turned stale.

When I'm lucky enough to recognize that the energy of a book is going bad, I force myself to stop reading because I know that if I don't, before long I'll start to feel an undertow, physical and psychic, sucking me under. With fiction, it's especially hard to let go—the magnetic force of a plot makes me want to stick around to see what happens—but the price is too high. I've paid it many a time. By the same token, all it takes is one sip of a good book—a paragraph or even a single sentence—and I start to feel like a flower in the rain; I drink the writing in, grateful for the new source of strength. *The Blind Masseuse* showed me how great the difference is between books that give energy and those that drain it away.

The thousands of hours I've spent reading because I needed to rest was what developed this radar. I became more and more sensitive to changes that, when I was well, I would never have noticed at all. Summertime on our deck in the mountains, winters on the seagrass sofa in Florida, reading became my primary form of experience. My husband would come home at night and I'd ask him about his day and he'd tell me the various things he'd done and then, when he asked me about mine, I would report on my reading. When a book had infused me with hope and strength, it literally made my day. I didn't actually tell him this because we are both former English professors and not accustomed to discussing books as if they were like chocolate mousse or a good massage.

But for me, whatever else books may be, they were, and are, an energy source. It's as if I've acquired a second, invisible body, called into existence by my illness. The etheric body knows what it likes and will feel alive and ready, or listless and weak, depending on the writer. I can feel joy and even bliss from reading a particular passage, and a book can cast me down into the pit and leave me there, sometimes for days.

That night on the sofa I went back and reread first one chapter of *The Blind Masseuse,* then another and another. I told myself that the reason I was rereading was in order to decipher the title's meaning and get straight the author's relationship with her boyfriend. In fact, I was reading for sustenance, for life-force—I wanted to spend more time with Alden Jones because being with her gave that to me. I remember one moment in particular. Alden has been helping to build a village school in Costa Rica. After bunking down for a month with several other people on the floor of a shack, she treats herself to a couple of nights in the San Jose Marriott, where she rents a room with a comfortable bed, TV, air-conditioning, and room service. She's hoping that her boyfriend, Andres, will show up. When she stops at the bar and gets a glass of white wine and, on her way up to the room, takes a sip, I can taste that wine and feel her enjoyment. When the chapter is over— Andres doesn't show; the chapter is about getting a massage from a blind man—I'm sorry, the way I am when I say good-bye to a friend.

Can books take the place of life? No. But it isn't a question of either/or. My illness taught me to recognize the value of books in a way I never did when I made my living by them teaching literature in college. As a university professor I'd come to regard my devotion to books as suspect because I saw that people who'd been drawn to scholarly pursuits (myself included) often used the intellectual realm, unconsciously, as a way to avoid facing both the world and themselves. I still think this is true, but I no longer believe that using books as a solace and a refuge is cowardly or a mistake. I was drawn to books in the first place, as a child, because they gave me the chance to experience the world at one remove—a distance I needed because the real world was often too assaultive for me to handle. And later, when contact with the world caused inner turmoil, books could soothe me, allow a breathing space, provide experiences that would neither threaten nor disturb; they could restore my faith in life and my ability to meet it face to face.

But despite all this, despite the nourishment and succor books have given me, and the precious taste of life they offer to me now, when people ask me what I'm writing about, I wish I didn't have to say "reading." I wish I could say that I was writing about my encounters with grizzlies in Alaska, or my foot journey across the Himalayas. It sounds more real and exciting. Perhaps this is because a forced passivity has made me hunger for excitement and adventure. Or perhaps it's because I've always believed Emerson's saying that books are for the scholar's idle times. Although I enjoyed the life of scholarship and teaching and was thoroughly committed to it, after I had reached a certain level of achievement, part of me wanted to leave the academy because I was afraid I was missing out on something. I wanted to use my body rather than my mind and be a producer rather than a consumer. On my second semester off in twenty-odd years I got a job at the local Whole Foods store and worked there as a breakfast cook for five months. It was hard but it was fun. I enjoyed working with my hands and being with people who didn't have college degrees. Still, even though I only worked on weekends, standing up for seven hours a day, stirring oatmeal in giant cauldrons, cutting up fruits and vegetables, searching for things in the giant freezers, and not getting in the way of the other cooks was exhausting. For the first time I understood why people go home and watch TV at the end of a workday. When you're that tired, it's all you can do.

But this book is not about adventures in the world because the only thing I've done much of for the last ten years is lie around and read. I read. I look out of windows. I'm friendly with the balconies and terraces of the building across the street from our apartment in New York; there's one planted with trees whose irregular outlines I love. Indoors, I gaze at pieces of furniture—the pale aqua easy chair and the orange Chinese chest; I appreciate their stability and enjoy noticing the way the light falls across them. I like the reflections off the glass of the watercolors on the walls, and the moody distance that stretches between me and the dining room table and chairs at the other end of the room. My husband and I live in three different places: the Catskill Mountains, New York City, and Florida. I'm attached to the rooms I've lain in in each of these places. Each one has sheltered me, afforded me rest, and given me some of its peace.

When I'm feeling relatively energetic, I sit: on a sofa, in a comfortable chair, sometimes at my computer desk, though that takes greater energy. Often I lie down. I lie on the bed—it's the most comfortable—though I don't like to lie there too much during the day because it makes me feel more like an invalid. I keep it for sleeping at night, napping, or reading myself to sleep during the day when I'm tired. But I live on the sofas. There I read, eat, do puzzles, talk on the phone, watch TV, curl up under a blanket, and doze off. If I'm lucky, Teddy, our black, long-haired half-Himalayan, will land on my chest, purr for a while, and sleep with me.

So, no, this book is not about climbing mountains or being in the wild, though it takes only a moment's reflection to see that in a way it is. Having a chronic illness that doctors don't understand, that does not kill you or go away, is a kind of wilderness adventure, one that would have driven me out of my mind or made me permanently depressed if I hadn't had books to read. I'm like the sickly boy in *The Secret Garden* who's forbidden to go out and play, until a young girl arrives on the scene and spirits him off to a beautiful walled garden where he learns to walk. For me, reading is a kind of secret garden that has kept me alive on the inside and connected me to the outer world.

But whether or not reading can actually be as thrilling as wilderness encounters must be largely a matter of temperament. As an English major, and an introvert, I've spent my share of delectable hours closeted with books, happy to be experiencing the world through the medium of print. Not everyone can. But the older I grow, the more I've come to feel that while reading about adventure can be thrilling, I'm even more keen to know what's going on inside the person who's having the adventure than I am to know about the adventure itself. The intimacy of self-disclosure draws me in a way that events alone rarely can. Isolation and inactivity turn one inward; the inner life starts to seem more real and more important than anything else, and the companionship of authors salves the need to be with other people, when actually doing so demands more energy than I have.

Inner Life

This morning I picked up a book that captivated me because, though it set out to be about travel, it ended up being about the author's inner life. The book was *The Art of Travel* by Alain de Botton. He's in London, it's November, the weather is awful, his mood despondent; he comes across a travel brochure showing palms on a beach, a blue ocean, azure sky. The next thing you know, he's got reservations for Barbados. His dream of escape from all that drags him down is about to be realized. But the chapter titled "On Anticipation" shows us how a traveler's actual experience is often dominated by things that have nothing to do with the pleasant vistas of a vacation spot. The author's digestive problems, boredom, worries about money, and being at odds with his partner simply take over—so much so, that he concludes it would have been easier and more pleasant to *imagine* himself in Barbados than to have actually made the trip. In de Botton's words: "it seems we may best be able to inhabit a place when we are not faced with the additional challenge of having to be there."

The first morning, he wakes up and goes to sit on the beach. He finds a deck chair right by the ocean, listens to the lapping sounds of waves, hears the birds excitedly chirping, recognizes the view from the brochure of a gently curving beach with jungle-covered hills rising behind it, and of course, the row of coconut palms leaning toward the sun.

> Yet this description only imperfectly reflects what occurred within me that morning.... My awareness was weakened by a number of other, incongruous and unrelated elements, among them a sore throat I had developed during the flight, worry over not having informed a colleague that I would be away, a pressure across both temples and a rising need to visit the bathroom. A momentous but until then overlooked fact was making itself apparent: I had inadvertently brought myself with me to the island.

I love this paragraph, which brings me in close to the writer, nearer than a film close-up could because one can't tell from a close-up that a person has a sore throat and needs to go to the bathroom. It's the self that the adventurer brings with him or her to the tropical island that engages me, and the intimacy I feel with the author when that self is revealed. When I know what's going on, on the inside, I identify, I sympathize, become more real to myself and exist more fully than I did the moment before. I'd rather have de Botton's description of his sore throat and needing to relieve himself than a series of heart-stopping escapades. Not that such adventures aren't exciting, but they don't have the allure of self-revelation.

Or perhaps it would be more accurate to say—the allure is different. In a memorable and engrossing account of walking across Afghanistan, *The Places in Between,* which I read around the same time as the book by Alain de Botton, Rory Stewart rarely describes his bodily sensations or his emotions though he had good reason to, since he ate poorly, suffered from intestinal disorders, walked through below-zero weather, and felt his life was being threatened more than once. The story is beautifully told, fascinating for its glimpses of life in Afghan villages and step-by-step description of traversing in winter the mountains and valleys that lie between Herat and Kabul. But it contains almost no introspection. The focus is out there on the mountains, the frozen river, the endless distances, or else on the cramped sleeping quarters and ancient social customs of the villages the writer bunks down in. To add interest and texture, Stewart quotes from the account of a similar journey: a conquest of Afghanistan by the Mughal emperor Babur, a charming and thought-provoking document—Babur is an excellent writer, though apparently he cut off a lot of heads. Stewart throws our attention outward into geography and history, where the issues are world-historical, externalized, and material. About himself he reveals practically nothing. And that is the draw. Seized by the vivid evocations of a far-off place and time, you can forget yourself completely. There's no inner consciousness to remind you of what might be going on in your own life. It's a vacation, all right, a vacation from your self.

I enjoyed Stewart's book and learned from it, but when the chips are down, it's the inner life I'm after. And the inner life can be just as intense as an account of conquests and beheadings. When de Botton describes how the sulk he was in, because of a fight with his partner over whose dessert was better, destroyed the effect of his beautiful hotel and the lovely tropical afternoon, I am just as riveted as I was when Stewart's life was threatened. In fact, more so. Perhaps because, after spending quite a bit of time thinking and writing about de Botton's inability to enjoy where he is because his inner weather didn't match the sunshine, it came to me that I had had exactly the same kind of experience—more than once—with the man who became my second husband. De Botton's vivid account of his feelings evoked an episode I'd long forgotten.

We'd gone to East Hampton for the weekend—neither of us had ever been there—and had reserved a room in an eighteenth-century inn (I had insisted on this); it was the last room available—in the attic, with no elevator and no air-conditioning. We sweltered under the low gable roof—my husband-to-be minded the heat even more than I did—and instead of making it into a joke or figuring out some alternative, we just lay there resenting the heat and each other. The whole weekend was like that: filled with sullen silences and, at least on my part, huge feelings of disappointment and discontent. Still, the weather was great. The beach was wide and the waves were good. We should have been happy. The truth was, I didn't want to be there with this man and couldn't admit it to myself. I thought our situation well characterized by the line from an old Protestant hymn: "Where every prospect pleases, / And only man is vile."

De Botton's quarrel over dessert reminded me of this failed vacation and also taught me something about how intimate self-revelation can be achieved and made to mean something. Which is to say, by recording the truth of a situation in microscopic detail and then stepping back from it in order to see its larger meaning: in his case, that emotional turmoil can blot out the loveliest of physical surroundings, and in mine, that I should not marry someone I didn't like going on vacations with (it happened again, on Martha's Vineyard, where we had, if anything, an even worse time).

But my point is not about vacations but about the power of inner experience to annihilate external events and surroundings.

De Botton actually got this idea from a book, J. K. Huysmans's *À rebours,* whose hero, Des Esseintes, spends his life surrounded by posters depicting vacation paradises in far-off places. He has discovered that the discomforts and tedium, mishaps and disappointments of travel can be avoided, and its pleasures savored in their purest form, by remaining at home and imagining all the wondrous sights and sensations the advertisements promise. De Botton makes Des Esseintes the pivot of his reflections on the time he spent in Barbados. Huysmans has given him the lens through which to see it: a literary lens made that experience available. He didn't just notice his sore throat, he noticed himself noticing it *and* not really paying any attention at all to the birds and the beach and the palm trees. Huysmans let him see what his situation really was, a combination of physical, emotional, and mental discomforts that canceled out the beauties and amenities of his surroundings. It was reading rather than travel that let him grasp the reality of his vacation.

Change

When it comes to that, the power of books to shape experience is not something most people would argue with. *À rebours* put words to a situation de Botton was in but hadn't previously been able to identify; it lit up his experience, enabling him to understand it. Never again would he set out for a tropical island expecting to be relieved of all worry and discomfort. Lives can be changed by books in myriad ways, especially if one is susceptible. They can make you not only *see* things, as de Botton did, but also *do* them.

Before the journey this book describes began, books had changed my life this way on three separate occasions—by which I mean, caused me to take action in the world, *new* action that altered my circumstances, though before I read de Botton reflecting on *À rebours* it had never been clear to me. Each time I made this kind of change in response to a book, it was for the same reason: I was dissatisfied with my life and looking for something different. In the first instance, I was recently divorced and living in Philadelphia. It was summer, and I was commuting every day to the library of the university where I taught—it involved taking two subways each way in the summer heat—where, in my soulless cubicle, I was trying to write an article on Richard Wright's *Black Boy* and spent quite a bit of time feeling miserable. As if to symbolize the general state of my affairs, I was also trying to grow grass in the sour-smelling soil of my backyard on Rodman Street—I lived in what's called a Father-Son-and-Holy-Ghost house, one room on each of three floors, and a kitchen in the basement. In my tiny yard I dug and fertilized and watered and sweated, and one day when I wasn't looking the grass appeared miraculously in thousands of thin lines of green, and then, just as suddenly, it died. It was around this time that I decided to reread Robert Pirsig's *Zen and the Art of Motorcycle Maintenance,* which had inspired and amazed me the first time I read it, in hopes that it would do the same thing again. This time, I became convinced that I should buy and learn to ride a motorcycle, something I had never contemplated before, and no small feat. I knew nothing of motorcycles or how to ride them or how dangerous they could be. I bought the motorcycle because (I told myself) I wanted to have the experience Pirsig had had of integrating the romantic and classic sides of his personality (the romantic side was riding the motorcycle, the classic side was fixing it). But the real reason was, I needed an adventure. I was about to get married to the wrong person (yes, it was the unhappy vacationer), and I needed something to spice up my life. Of course I didn't know this at the time.

I signed up for a class in motorcycle riding which took place evenings in a parking lot on the outskirts of the city. Though it took a lot more nerve than I possessed, when my turn came, I managed to get on a bike and do what I was told. At night lying in bed after each lesson, immobile, and terrified at what I had done, I discovered the meaning of the expression "stiff with fright." But I learned to ride and bought a Honda CB200, the smallest street bike with a four-cycle engine I could find—I had to be able to set it upright if it went down—silver and black and beautifully proportioned, and I rode it to work from Center City to North Philadelphia and back every day. I was frightened of it and I loved it and it made me feel like an urban cowboy: mobile, sexy, a little tough, and able to make a fast getaway. This was mostly in my head. Riding down Eleventh Street in North Philly on my way home from school one day, I was mugged by a group of boys gathered at an open fire hydrant. I didn't get away all that fast: they tore the watch from my wrist and my handbag, containing a set of student papers, from the back of the motorcycle, but I held on to the bike. Just in time, the car ahead of me, which had been stopped for a light, moved forward and I gunned the motor, praying I wouldn't run anybody over, and zoomed away. I got home, shaken. Still, the bike served its purpose. I had conquered my fear of riding—I hadn't anticipated being mugged—and when my body felt the vibration of the wheels through the soft leather of the seat—a titillating, satisfying feeling—I knew I was alive.

Reading can be a compensatory activity and an escape, but it can also lead you into the world rather than away from it. This kind of reading, reading that has agency in one's life, plays a dynamic rather than a pacifying role. The book becomes a catalyst, a crystallizer of desire and an instrument of realization. I never would have bought and learned to ride a motorcycle if I hadn't read Pirsig's book. That experience, which I treasure despite its scary aspects, was his gift to me.

One husband and four decades later, retired, sick, and once more needing to jump-start my life, I read another book that made me take action in the world. The book was *Noah's Garden:*

Restoring the Ecology of Our Own Back Yards by Sara Stein. This is not just another gardening book. Like Pirsig, Stein is an eloquent writer, passionately committed to her project, which is to bring back disappearing wildlife by restoring the plant communities that support it—communities that development has destroyed. Rather than just railing at the wholesale destruction of native plants in the settled portions of the United States, Stein gives you something to do about it. But first she makes you cry.

Stein had grown up in the Massachusetts countryside, and when she moved back there as an adult discovered that the wildlife she'd loved as a youngster—the moles, the voles, the field mice, the foxes, the frogs, the toads, the dragonflies and butterflies—had almost disappeared. The book records her efforts to find out why and to do something about it. She explains: when the agricultural practices of America's European settlers had robbed the soil of its productivity, the farmers moved west; and as suburbs moved in, what farming hadn't done away with, the three-hundred-year-old tradition of the British lawn finished off. All over the country, in place of the vast variety of native trees and grasses, flowers, bushes, and weeds that once were there, we now have the shaven lawns of Oxford, chemically treated, where nothing can live. But what Stein's book shows its readers is that rather than wait for a change of consciousness in our culture regarding foreign vs. native plants or the passage of new legislation, people can begin to bring back what was banished by replanting their own backyards. After explaining what makes the native habitat so important—for example, caterpillars can't eat the leaves of non-native trees, and without caterpillars, birds can't feed their young—Stein tells the reader how to plant for birds and butterflies and the myriad creatures that support life up and down the food chain: how to create a wetland, how to grow a woodland, how to plant a prairie, in your yard.

This was perfect for me. Because of my illness, which had gotten worse—hence, my retirement—I couldn't work, volunteer, exercise, or even socialize much. There seemed no way for me to feel productive, and, therefore, worthwhile. But we were about to landscape the property around our house in Delray Beach, and I did have a say over what would happen there. It was within my power to bring a small plot of earth back to something resembling original conditions, a garden where animals, birds, and insects could thrive.

Physically, I couldn't do the work, and landscapers in that locale don't know much about native plants, but I found one who was willing to learn and together we figured it out. Well, he figured it out, and I contributed information gleaned from Rufino Osorio's *Gardener's Guide to Florida's Native Plants.* Restoring my own backyard, like motorcycle riding, was a steep learning curve, but things grow fast in Florida; the garden flourished and was beautiful. Besides providing a lush retreat, it nourished me in the making: planning for it introduced me to the flora of the coastal hammock where I lived, and taught me to identify native trees and plants. As I took visitors through the garden I delighted in being able to name them all. The visitors soon grew bored, but the animals liked it. One day sitting by the pond, I saw a long black shadow falling across the ground where a shadow had never been. I looked at the tree branches above me; I looked for the angle of the sun: this shadow made no sense. Then it came to me: it's not a shadow, it's a snake. And so it was. I made myself concentrate on something else, and, five or ten minutes later I looked again and it was gone. The gardener told me later we had two blacksnakes living in the yard. So the mockingbirds and blacksnakes, dragon-flies and frogs, butterflies, toads, geckos, neighborhood cats and, naturally, rats, and probably a lot of other creatures I never saw, all came. That book I read provided them with a home and me with a raison d'être for seven years.

This story has a coda and a moral. Eventually we sold the

house: it was too much to keep up. Our realtor talked us into selling to a builder who was representing a third party. Despite her assurances that the builder would only remodel, not rebuild, I knew it was bad idea, but I gave in. The house was razed, and the garden destroyed completely: every vine, every bush, every tree, every plant, the pond, the decks, the walkways. Nothing remained. After I got over the initial shock and hurt, the experience taught me this: that the process of making something is as important, perhaps more important, than the thing that is made. Causing the garden to be, day by day, had given me a connection to life that I badly needed. Spending time with my landscaper, of whom I grew fond, visiting native plant preserves and nurseries, poring over Rufino Osorio, walking in the garden every day to see how the plants were doing, and making plans for what to do next, gave me something worthwhile to do that was within my capabilities at a time when it seemed that nothing else was. Although, like everyone I know, I am object-oriented and product-driven, the destruction of the garden has let me realize in hindsight the value of the slow forward and backward movement of creation, the sustenance provided by having a goal and inching toward it over time; the loss has made me aware of the way that making something entangles you with the world, opens up relations between you and it, its materials, its people, its modes of operation. I wasn't aware of this when I was making the garden; I just believed in it and what it stood for, and standing for this belief gave me a sense of purpose at a time when I periodically wondered whether there was any point in being alive at all. A book that gives you something to believe in and something to do about it—its price is greater than rubies.

Reading can bring about the same sort of entanglement with life that creation does by waking you up to possibilities of action and experience you hadn't known existed.

Halfway between the motorcycle and the garden, I read the

third book that changed my life materially and spiritually; it offered me a different sort of cause and a way to implement it, one that transformed the way I taught and eventually the way I lived—Paulo Freire's *Pedagogy of the Oppressed*. Freire was a Brazilian educator and philosopher influenced by Catholic liberation theology. He taught in a situation completely different from mine. His aim was revolution. In a country run by a military dictatorship, he was attempting to enable peasants to realize that they had the right to control their own lives through self-government. But it was clear to him that democracy was not something that could be taught merely by talking about it. The very process of learning what they needed to know in order to take control of their lives had to embody the goal. The teacher-student relationship could not mirror the relationship between oppressor and oppressed. Students had to become agents of their own liberation. You can't liberate another person, Freire said, people have to learn to liberate themselves; or, in the sentence that went off like firecracker the first time I read it: "education must become a practice of freedom." I have never recovered.

The reason Freire hit me so hard was that for quite a while I'd been dissatisfied with what was going on in my own classroom. Not much was coming from the students sitting in rows before me; I seemed to be doing all the work. My ideal classroom was one where the students would be on fire with their own ideas, barely able to restrain themselves while they listened to the others talking. As I stood up there in front of them, trying to get the material across, I felt an absence of energy on their part. And no wonder. Despite my vision of excited universal participation, as a teacher I was chiefly preoccupied with whether I'd appear knowledgeable, intelligent, and well-prepared. It wasn't that I didn't love my subject matter or care about my students; I just didn't know how to engage them. I thought the burden was on me to perform in so spectacular a way that the students couldn't fail to be interested in the texts I'd assigned. Night after night I stayed up late preparing my classes, putting everything I had into it, trying to present the material in a way that was accurate, comprehensive, cutting-edge, and compelling. But it was hit or miss. Sometimes it worked, more often it didn't. And, it was tiring. Freire changed all that.

From reading his book, I came to see that students were not empty vessels into which knowledge could be poured at regular intervals. They did not have to be coaxed, like kindling, into bursting into flame. Through experiment, I discovered that students were already on fire, that they were walking fields of energy, teeming with agendas. All I had to do was figure out how to tap that energy and elicit those agendas, and the best way to do that turned out to be to get out of the way. I stopped standing in front of the classroom and put the students there instead, gave them the responsibility for teaching the material to the other students, and in some instances for coming up with the assignments. This led to our stepping away from the classroom altogether, or transforming it, into environments that would deepen our understanding of the subject in ways that talking about it never could. My field was American literature. But instead of spending all our time poring over the meaning of a particular text, we used the text as a springboard for getting to know the world. Thoreau didn't want people to spend their time analyzing his relationship to nature. He wanted people to know nature for themselves. Melville didn't care about theories of epistemology as applied to *Moby-Dick;* he wanted his readers to feel and see what he had from the deck of a whaling ship. So we went on walks, paddled down a river, climbed a small mountain, spent time on an old plantation (this was when we read Toni Morrison's *Beloved*), and visited the sea. Freirean student-centered education turned into experiential learning. Knowledge, I learned, comes in through all the senses; and it comes through emotional experience; there are many pathways through which people can be changed, and through which they can express what they know. The things I did in response to Freire's book changed me.

What takes place when a person reads a book, though you can neither see nor touch it, is the opposite of insignificant: it is the interplay of human souls. And while it's true that, whatever his subject, every writer writes of himself, the self-revelation is not all one-way. The reader is defined by the way she reads as much as the author is by the way she writes. I never learned to fix a motorcycle because of reading Pirsig, but another person would have. If you look at how you're responding to the book in your hand, you'll see that your response is telling its own story—about you. Books bring things out in us that real-life experiences don't. Books are developmental. They cause changes to take place within. Books can get you to change your hairdresser; they can make you leave your spouse. Or—and this is more along the lines I'm pursuing here—they can let you see what kind of person you are, or were, or want to, and still can, be.

1

The Gift

I was in Florida when I received the book. We were moving. The house—built in 1948, a block from the beach—was too much to take care of, and, though I didn't like to admit it, the garden took its toll. I loved the house and garden. They were full of charm. But we weren't up to it anymore. It was time.

We'd hired someone to help us sort through our belongings— keep it, sell it, give it away—Patty could get rid of anything in a trice. One day she asked her sister to take her place. It was the day I was supposed to go through my files, what remained of my career as a teacher and writer. Contrary to expectation, Maggie wouldn't let me throw away much. She'd been a lawyer on Wall Street for twenty-three years, been married to a professor of screenwriting at NYU. After he died, people had wanted his papers, and that made her think someone might want mine. It was flattering, if unrealistic. Sitting in my study, talking about what to keep and what to let go of, we got to know one another; I lent her a copy of my memoir, *A Life in School.* A week later, Maggie sent me a book in return. The book was *Sir Vidia's Shadow* by Paul Theroux.

Sir Vidia's Shadow is a memoir of the friendship between Theroux, a well-known American novelist and nonfiction writer, and V. S. Naipaul, a Trinidadian author of East Indian descent who won the Nobel Prize for literature in 2001. Not the sort of book one would expect to have life-changing consequences. I was about to go on a week's vacation in Italy and thought I'd glance at the book before leaving, just to confirm my belief that it wouldn't interest me. I'd never read anything by Theroux and had a negative impression of Naipaul, based on a piece of his I'd read in the *New Yorker.*

I was wrong about the book. When I opened it, I was hooked immediately. I read it on the nine-and-a-half-hour flight from New York to Frankfurt, and then on the flight from Frankfurt to Bari. I read it in Italy—I had plenty of time since I had to take every other day off from the rigors of the tour we were on; it was the first time I'd been able to travel for many years—and I finished it on the way back to the States. This was not airplane reading—not an action-adventure story or a tender romance; it was a memoir, but not about recovery from a breakdown or overcoming a great obstacle. It was about a thirty-year friendship between two men. One did not save the other from drowning, they didn't have sex with each other or each other's wives, or try to wreck one another's careers. They wrote letters back and forth, had lunch, and went on the occasional excursion. I couldn't put it down. And when I finished it, I wanted to read it again. I wanted to remain within the aura of the book. And I wanted to discover why it fascinated me so.

I'm an enthusiast when it comes to books. If I read one that moves me, I tell all my friends about it and will sometimes give it as a gift to the unsuspecting. This book was different. It had reached inside and grabbed me where I lived, gotten into my system like an allergy or an infection. But I didn't know why. What had made me susceptible?

The first thing I thought of was the style. In falling for *Sir Vidia's Shadow,* I was answering an old call. I had written my doctoral dissertation on Melville's prose style. Hearing passages from *Moby-Dick* read aloud to two hundred undergraduates by one of my graduate school professors, I thought I'd never heard anything so powerful, and here it was again, the spell of language brilliantly deployed. In *Sir Vidia's Shadow* every word is held in place by one magnetic force, an invisible current that charges every scene. The current, the lifeblood, controls the narrative structure as well as the shapes of sentences and paragraphs; its energy is tremendous. Reading it made me want to plunge into that invisible current and start writing myself, if only to find out what it was that had turned me on.

During the first two years of retirement I'd written two essays, one about learning, the other about playing the piano. I'd tried to write other things as well, but nothing took. My head wanted me to write, but body and spirit did not. Instead, I tinkered at the piano in the winter, and in the summer I began to paint. But now, after seven years, suddenly it took no effort to sit down at my desk and write.

Theroux explains in an afterword that he did not compose from notes or diaries but from recall. Long swatches of dialogue; detailed descriptions of countryside, interiors, meals eaten twenty years ago; what people wore, the expressions on their faces, the jokes they told—it all came to him unbidden. The details, the moments, are charged with the urgency of things that have to be said; the rhythm and sequence of the sentences communicate this. The sentences seem shot from guns, taut and targeted. There are no flourishes or special effects. With the book's focused forward movement, always covering ground, the style conforms to one of Sir Vidia's maxims: never let your language call attention to itself. Theroux writes exactly as his mentor might have wished: he stays close to the ground, hews to particulars. He makes his points without stating them. The question is: what made these memories so vivid for him: why does he not need a single prompt? And why, whenever I picked the book up, could I not put it down? Was it only the writing?

Here's a passage. Theroux, Naipaul, and his wife, Pat, are seated at the Kaptagat Arms, a hotel in northern Kenya. Political unrest has driven them out of Kampala, the capital of Uganda, where Vidia and Paul first met. They both had appointments at Makerere University, Vidia as a visiting author, Paul as a member of the faculty. In this scene they've just learned that the hotel is about to close. This upsets Pat, who starts to cry. Then, "'Oh, my, Vidia, look,' she said, and gestured towards a waiter. 'His poor shoes.'"

> They were broken, without laces, the counters crushed, the tongues missing, the heels worn. . . . The sight of the shoes reduced Pat to tears once again. Each time she saw the man wearing them, she began to sob. I did not tell her that Africans got such shoes second- and third-hand. . . . The shoes, like the torn shirts and torn shorts they wore, were often merely symbolic.
>
> "Don't be sad, Patsy," Vidia said. "He'll be all right. He'll go back to his village. He'll have his bananas and his bongos. He'll be frightfully happy." (53)

Theroux doesn't say a word about what he thinks this scene reveals. Though it says a great deal about Pat, about Vidia's attitude toward her and, even more, toward Africans, and about the author's relationship to both of them, Theroux doesn't comment; he moves on, letting the evidence mount. Here, and in the book as a whole, you feel a case is being made, but what case? Is it about the kind of person Naipaul is? Is it about the author's position in relation to Naipaul? Is it about writing as a profession? The exact nature of the agenda isn't clear. A case is being made, the evidence is accumulating, but the facts veer this way and that. They point in different directions. To figure out what's really being said in this memoir of a friendship you have to keep reading till the end. But after I got to the end I still had questions: what is it Theroux wants us to believe about his friend? What are we supposed to make of the way he portrays himself? Why, when I read this book, did I feel like an old war horse whose blood jumps when he hears the bugle sound? Why did the relationship between the young writer and the better-known, older writer seem so important to me? Why were the stakes so high?

When I first read the book, the mainspring of Theroux's account seemed to be the divide between Naipaul's life and his work. I was familiar with the proposition. The memoir I'd given Maggie was an attempt to understand the relationship between my life as a human being who caught colds, took showers, drank orange juice, and had desires, and the person who taught American literature and literary theory to college students. Long and hard I'd struggled to overcome this divide, to integrate who I was as a human being into my work as a writer and a teacher: the chasm between life and work had been what my experimental teaching was all about. I could quote from memory the lines from Yeats that state the dilemma so succinctly:

The intellect of man is forced to choose
Perfection of the life, or of the work,
And if it choose the second must refuse
A heavenly mansion, raging in the dark.

Yeats thought of himself, I'm sure, as having made the choice for work. I thought of myself the same way. The split I believed Theroux was pointing to in Naipaul conformed to one of the templates I carried in my brain. Perhaps this was why I was so drawn to the story of the two writers. The facts of Naipaul's life seemed to fit the pattern. He is, on the one hand, a gifted author, uncompromisingly devoted to his craft, who rises from humble beginnings in a far-off colonial possession and wins a knighthood and then the Nobel Prize on the basis of his writing. On the other hand, he is a husband who—in scenes like the one just described and in several others—patronizes and neglects his wife, a man who, in the course of the narrative, mistreats servants, bad-mouths other writers, views most of humanity as his inferiors, and takes advantage of the kindness of his friends. But although the outlines of Naipaul's story conform to the art-life dichotomy, Theroux doesn't interpret the facts that way. Vidia's transgressions, his crankiness, his downright meanness to others, are never attributed to the pressures of his work. If anything, in Theroux's eyes, Naipaul's literary ambition and his mistreatment of others stem from an overpowering need to feel superior. It's not workaholism or fanatic perfectionism that get him into trouble, it's an uncontrollable desire for self-aggrandizement. When Theroux addresses this issue late in the book, he attributes Naipaul's megalomania to insecurity. Whatever harm Naipaul may have done, devotion to his craft was not responsible.

And besides, Theroux doesn't understand his own life in those terms. He never sets up an opposition between his work and his personal life. On the contrary, he makes a point of the ease with which, as a young man at Makerere University, he teaches, writes, socializes with his colleagues, and has pleasurable, guiltless sex with African women—all in the course of a normal day. Life and work are shown flowing peacefully side by side. Later, when Theroux struggles to support a family on his meager earnings as a writer, he never sees the two aspects of his life as getting in the way of each other. He even offers us a halcyon description of how well they dovetail in his account of living with his family and writing in a Victorian house in London. I had to abandon this view of the memoir. The art-life opposition was an import from my own life, superimposed. Theroux does not suggest it. There must have been another reason the book had cast its spell on me.

What was it, then?

In the end, the nasty Naipaul, the one we don't like, cuts the tie with Theroux—his friend, confidant, and disciple of thirty years—and cuts it with terrible swiftness, offering no explanation.

Theroux's depiction of the moment when Naipaul rejects him is so powerful that it's traumatic to read. Yet when I came to this scene at the end of the memoir, what impressed me the most about it was that Theroux does not make Naipaul the scapegoat. This is not a vengeful book. Beneath the surface of the story you can feel Theroux's hurt, anger, and resentment—the extraordinary intensity of the scenes is owing no doubt to their presence—but by and large Theroux lets the events he narrates speak for themselves, leaves us to interpret the images, makes no comment even on something as startling as "bananas and bongos." Of course you could say that this is just a stratagem. It's Theroux, after all, who's decided what to include and what to leave out, who gets to frame every incident, color the details, and provide a context. He can get us to see Naipaul any way he wants through emphasis, omission, or insinuation. If he alters the facts or fails to tell us something crucial, we'll be none the wiser. But I never felt that there was any conscious manipulation of the facts on Theroux's part. It may only be testimony to his guile or to my gullibility, but for me the genius of the book lies in its refusal to take sides. Theroux consistently gives the impression that he is being faithful to events as they occurred, as faithful as it was possible for him to be.

The scene that established for me this extraordinary evenhandedness is the one where you would least expect to find it, the one in which Naipaul destroys their friendship. Theroux's depiction of the moment when Naipaul rejects him manages to transcend questions of right and wrong. The fierceness of the event and the intensity with which it is presented are such that one refrains from saying, "This is bad, this shouldn't have happened." It just is.

The scene takes place in London. Theroux, who now lives between Hawaii and Cape Cod, is there for a week's book promotion, and his son, whom he calls Marcel, has just arrived at his hotel for a visit. Theroux is obsessed with doubt about his relationship to Naipaul, not having heard from him in over a year, and has been stung recently by a fax he's received from Naipaul's new wife, Nadira (Pat has died and Naipaul has remarried). Written in a loopy, childish hand, brimming with embarrassing mistakes in style and grammar, it contains one insult after another, the worst insult being Nadira's criticism of the obituary Paul had written for Pat, at Vidia's request, which Vidia had thanked him for pointedly by mail more than once. Paul reasons that Vidia must not have known about this fax, so he had faxed a copy of it back to Naipaul with questions, but has heard nothing from him. Now, in London, Theroux can't contain his anxiety. He walks down the Gloucester Road with Marcel, gabbling, forcing his son to listen as he goes over and over the same issues—Naipaul mustn't have known about the insulting fax, his wife must have intercepted Theroux's messages, she must have kept Naipaul in the dark—when all of a sudden, as they are walking, Naipaul appears on the pavement thirty feet away. He doesn't recognize Theroux and Marcel. Theroux imagines he and his son might appear to Naipaul at a distance to be potential Paki-bashers, ready to attack a small dark man in tweeds alone on the street with nobody to back him up. When finally Theroux addresses him and Naipaul looks up—"Paul!"—awkward words ensue. Naipaul mutters that he's on his way to the park to take a walk after lunch. He tries to move away. Theroux struggles to detain him with a question about the book Naipaul is working on and, when Naipaul seems to be escaping, asks if he's received a fax.

> "Yes. Now I must—"
> "Do we have something to discuss?"
> "No." He had almost broken away. He was moving crabwise, crouching a bit, cramming his hat down.
> "What do we do, then?"

He drew his mouth back. His face went darker. His mouth twisted down. It was the look of helpless suffering he wore the very first time I saw him in Uganda. His fingers on his cane went pale and prehensile.

"Take it on the chin and move on."

The moment toward which the book has been heading since the opening sentence has been reached: the friendship is over. Naipaul refuses to talk about it. His final words, though harsh, are in keeping with other pieces of wisdom he has offered at moments of crisis: "you have to leave her," "problems are good." Moreover, he's right. There's nothing else for Theroux to do but take it on the chin and move on. Even at the bitterest moment—and from Theroux's description of his face, we know it is bitter for Naipaul as well as for Theroux—Naipaul retains his cutting precision and strength of personality. He still controls the situation.

The greatness of Theroux's achievement comes through in this scene because he gives Naipaul his due even as Naipaul is cutting him off. Naipaul's virtues and defects are present simultaneously: monster and weakling, truth-teller and stalwart. At this moment, when the picture of Naipaul is complete, he seems beyond judgment. We know the circumstances of Naipaul's life as Theroux has given them to us—his struggles as a writer in perpetual exile, his accomplishments, his vanity, his kindness to Theroux, his disdain for other people, his shabby treatment of his first wife and subjection to his second. More than any of these things, we know what the friendship means to Paul. And yet, although it ends with Vidia's committing a kind of psychological murder—he stabs the friendship to death right there in the street—Vidia is still noble. As he disappears from view, it's as though he has ascended into the heavens to become a constellation like a figure from a Greek myth—beyond our capacity to lay a hand on him.

There is one more twist to the plot. A paragraph of unflattering description follows in which Theroux makes Naipaul seem diminutive, a parody of his old self as he scuttles toward the Kensington Road, growing smaller and smaller, and finally seeming to become his own shadow. It's as if Theroux needed to take his hurt out on Naipaul, at least for a few minutes, before letting him go. And then Theroux rallies. He turns the rejection into a liberation.

> I was dazed because I was liberated at last. I saw how the end of a friendship was the start of an understanding. He had made me his by choosing me; his rejection of me meant I was on my own, out of his shadow. He had freed me. He had opened my eyes, he had given me a subject.
>
> Before we got to the Cromwell Road I had begun this book in my head, starting at the beginning. That is everything.

These are the book's final words. Having just received a devastating blow from his lifelong friend, instead of allowing himself to be wiped out by it, Theroux, in a gesture of bravado, claims that he's the one who has the upper hand. Naipaul, far from injuring him by depriving him of his friendship, has given him a subject for another book. And then Theroux adds, referring to the book he's going to write, "That is everything."

Really? Is being able to write yet another in a long line of books worth losing one of his most important relationships? Can all that happens to a writer be dealt with by becoming material? Theroux is saving face here but in doing so lets us glimpse the monster in himself. After Naipaul has dealt the coup de grâce, Theroux doesn't miss a beat before turning his cherished friendship into a source of productivity, grist for the mill—*nulla die sine linea* (no day without a line)—a questionable bargain in personal terms, but for the reader, a stroke of luck. *Sir Vidia's Shadow* is probably his best book.

I was so affected by the scene that I had to know more about these men. Forget life vs. art. The fierceness of the final scene between Naipaul and Theroux, as Theroux presents it to us, blasts through such distinctions. There's an inevitability in the moment that testifies to some truth. Trying to understand the truth of that moment, I felt there was something here, just below the surface of the relationship between the two men, that could help me live my own life.

I knew from *Sir Vidia's Shadow* that Theroux's relationship to Naipaul was based on their both being writers, Theroux, at first, the aspiring beginner, Naipaul the well-published, well-respected man of letters. Their correspondence deals with literary matters—Naipaul gives Theroux advice, praise, encouragement, and practical help. He puts Theroux in touch with the editor of the *Times Literary Supplement* so he can become known on the London scene through writing book reviews. Theroux, for his part, introduces Naipaul to his publisher and writes a full-length critical study of Naipaul's work to introduce him to an American audience. We learn about their habits—Naipaul found composition laborious and exhausting; his wife, Pat, typed his manuscripts for him and offered shrewd criticism; Theroux composed on a typewriter, sitting in cramped rooms in rented quarters; to recharge he would take walks, go grocery shopping, visit the local pub. We find out how they supported themselves, Naipaul by writing articles and reviews for magazines and newspapers (anything to keep from having to teach), Theroux by teaching at first and then by following Naipaul's example once he became well enough known. We follow them from London to the English countryside, writing in places where they can afford to live. Both are peripatetic—traveling the world, basing novels, books of social commentary, and travel narratives on the culture and geography of the countries they visit. It all seems adventurous and romantic, the writer's life.

Because for me theirs had been a road not taken, I wanted to know more. I wanted to know what it would have been like to live outside of institutions, work devotedly at a craft, to travel and to write. I wanted to know what kinds of mistakes they'd made, what motivated them. Now that I look back on it, it might have made more sense to have consulted biographical material, but instead, I went to their work for answers. I didn't want my impressions to be filtered through another person's consciousness. And besides, I believe the clichés are true. The style is the man. Whoever puts pen to paper writes of himself. I didn't know it then, but it was going to take a long time to answer these questions, and longer still to discover why Theroux's account of their relationship had affected me so deeply. But time was what I had.

2

Literary Criticism

I wanted to know more about Naipaul and Theroux, but at Yale, where I went for my doctorate in English, you didn't dare show any interest in the author of a literary work, much less any interest in how the work had affected you. Interest in the author as a human being was considered a doctrinal error and in poor taste; interest in oneself was simply unthinkable. What Yeats called "the blood and mire of human veins" had no place in the business we were learning.

I'd been taught that literary studies should be conceived as a scientific enterprise, intent upon describing the structure and content of literary works with the same rigor and objectivity that investigators brought to bear upon a specimen in a laboratory. You weren't supposed to dig around in an author's biography trying to psych out what kind of person he was, or look for tidbits that might throw light on his work. *The Road to Xanadu,* by John Livingstone Lowes, a famous book that marshaled an exhaustive collection of sources attempting to identify the origins of Coleridge's most famous poems, "Kubla Khan" and "The Rime of the Ancient Mariner," was roundly ridiculed. Nor was there any room for imaginative flights, such as essays on "the girlhood of Cordelia," which my Shakespeare professor referred to with withering disdain, or for enthusiastic appreciations of poetic beauty like the short essays introducing the metaphysical poets in an anthology we used in my Renaissance literature course—appreciations my

Renaissance professor considered beneath contempt (I thought they were wonderful). Imagination and emotion were just as forbidden as recourse to history and biography. For someone like me, this went against the grain, but I trusted my professors and believed what they said. And the goal was fair enough: to keep literary criticism from seeming impressionistic and subjective by fixing the object of study and defining the methods of approaching it in a rigorous manner. The hope was that literary studies could then compete with physics and chemistry for academic prestige. It was the post-Sputnik era.

By shutting itself off from so many things, the New Criticism, as it was called, assured its own downfall. The landscape of literary criticism has changed drastically since then: myth criticism, psychoanalytic criticism, Marxist criticism, structuralist criticism, poststructuralist criticism (sometimes called deconstruction), new historicism, feminist criticism, queer theory, race theory, postcolonial theory, and personal criticism have all had their day, and many have disappeared. I'd been involved in several of these movements, and more have arisen since that I'm not familiar with. But the New Criticism, for all its flaws, taught those of us who grew up under its sway something invaluable: the technique of close reading. This meant the ability to analyze a piece of writing, word by word and line by line, pressing hard on the details of the text so as to miss nothing that they might suggest or imply. It meant parsing the syntax of sentences, the structure of paragraphs, the shapes of stanzas and chapters, to see how the parts were related to each other, with parts often seen—figures of speech, especially—as emblems of the whole. It meant cultivating the faculty of seeing what lay beneath the surface features of a text by looking closely at the surface features themselves. I would not trade this training for anything. And when I realized that I was interested mainly in the men behind the works I was now reading, and somewhat less in the works themselves, I began to feel defensive and apologetic.

As I penetrated further into the works of Naipaul and Theroux, I found myself taking liberties with another person's psyche, making guesses about his probable motivations and judgments about his behavior; I couldn't escape the feeling that I oughtn't to be doing it. I was writing about Naipaul in the way I might speculate with a friend about someone we both knew, and praising or blaming (but usually blaming) him for being a certain kind of person. It felt illegitimate, and it was also fun, the way gossip is fun.

I first began to think out loud about the kind of person Naipaul was while sitting with Maggie at the Côté France, a French bakery in a shopping center in Boca Raton, all tasteful plantings, brick paving, ochre stucco, and Mediterranean roof tiles. The people who ran the bakery spoke French, and sometimes there were French-speaking people at the other tables. It was as close to a Parisian café as you can get in South Florida. We sat outdoors under the arches of a handsome loggia and talked away the afternoon.

Maggie, a corporate attorney, had read deeply and steadily and had recently started to write a novel of her own. Having grown up with alcoholic parents and a father who beat her mother, she'd decided to see if writing a novel about it could help her in coming to terms with that experience. The novel, already well-launched, was wrenching, and written as if she'd been writing all her life. Every Monday we'd meet at the Côté France and give each other feedback on what we'd written. Having given me *Sir Vidia's Shadow,* Maggie had come up with a copy of Naipaul's first major novel, *A House for Mr. Biswas.* And we went to town. We talked mainly about Naipaul's gynophobia and his elitism. This bothered me. It seemed all we were doing was saying things about another person behind his back, a practice that in real life I tried to stay away from. I'd long ago come to believe that literary criticism often boils down to nothing more than the critic making himself feel better by finding fault with someone else—either the author or another critic, usually the latter. I thought it oughtn't to be that way, and now I was doing it myself. When we sat in the loggia we were always going for the weakness. Who or what was being served by this? It wasn't the personal nature of what we said that bothered me so much, it was the sharp critical edge.

In graduate school the point was to show that you could read a text with discernment, respond to the nuances of language, read between the lines, draw parallels, reveal hitherto unseen depths. You did this in order to arrive at a new interpretation of the text, one which had never been thought of until you came along. This kind of criticism, which I'd practiced when I started out, had nothing wrong with it. The difficulty was that sooner or later it became a vehicle for displaying your superior intelligence, insight, and scholarly acumen in the guise of revealing the truth about a literary work.

But I wasn't trying to write literary criticism. What I was doing was something else. I had started by asking a question: why does this book, *Sir Vidia's Shadow,* have such power over me? It was to learn about the author and about myself at the same time that I had embarked on this journey. I was not doing literary criticism in the usual sense. I hadn't written anything in a long time, and now that I was well enough to write, I didn't want to do it in an academic vein anymore. This wasn't a professional undertaking: the aim was understanding, and I was doing it for myself. I wanted to see what I could learn, and do it for the sheer pleasure of doing it. I wasn't trying to position myself intellectually, claim new territory, or set myself up against a reigning dogma. I wasn't trying to place myself in relation to other people who had written about Naipaul and Theroux. My questions about these men were pressing because in some way they reflected concerns I had about my own life. I didn't recognize this fully at the outset, or for some time thereafter, but slowly and painstakingly, I did recognize it. Meanwhile, for years nothing had piqued my interest the way *Sir Vidia's Shadow* had. And now Maggie had produced her copy of one of Naipaul's well-known novels, *A House for Mr. Biswas.* I was being given a chance at something and I wanted to take it.

3

Frustration and Discontent

A House for Mr. Biswas is a hard-bitten account of life in Trinidad among the immigrant Indian population where Naipaul grew up. Based on the life of the novelist's father, it's an early work and said to be one of Naipaul's best. I found it gripping but abrasive. Still, it was readable, so I soldiered on. The highly detailed, sometimes labored, descriptions of life in an extended Indian family—where they slept, what they wore, who did the washing and the cooking, who gave the orders, what the pecking order was—turn into an indictment of life on the island as a whole, or indeed, life in general. Nothing ever goes right for the protagonist in *Biswas,* or at least, very rarely. Satisfaction is to be found neither in the country nor the city, neither at home nor at work. Mr. Biswas's marriage is an accident—one day he gets up the courage to write a love note to a daughter of the family whose store he's working in, a girl he doesn't know, and in no time her family has chosen him as her husband. Her family has the note he sent her, he can't get out of the marriage, and since he's unable to support a family on his own, he becomes dependent for food and lodging on her powerful relations.

A feeling of fatality and the limits of existence dominates everything in the story. The texture of life is bleak—the food he eats doesn't give Biswas any pleasure, the island scenery produces problems and irritation for him, never joy. His marriage seems neither meaningful nor happy—he just accepts it. All around him there is suffering and deprivation: his mother lives in an unpainted shack with his crippled brother, who lies in a dark room until the day he dies. Wealth is usually seen as wasted on those who have it. Biswas has no friends to speak of. Living conditions, no matter where he is, are cramped and uncomfortable (Biswas's desire for a house of his own provides the impetus for the plot). His only pleasures are smoking cigarettes and writing. After several stabs at earning a living in a variety of frustrating menial jobs, he finally finds work writing for a newspaper but still doesn't make enough money to buy a house.

At one point, Biswas takes his family on a vacation. They drive to the other side of the island and stay in a rented house for a week. Initially, there's a sense of buoyancy and relief. As the family drive toward their destination in their new car, there's the hope that finally someone in this novel is going to have a good time. But no. The wind is too strong, the sun too bright, there's nothing to do. Nature, as usual, frustrates human intentions. The whole thing fizzles.

At the end of the story, Biswas finds a house that looks promising. From the outside it looks cozy and inviting, and, when he visits, the inside seems homey and attractive as well. He's been looking for a house for a long time with no success. The price is something he can just manage to afford, and recently he, his wife, and four children have been crowded into one room in the family compound. It seems a great opportunity, so he jumps at it. But the house is not what he thought. It's a furnace during the day, the bathroom is poorly located, the staircase is on the outside, other spaces are ill-arranged, and so on. The discomforts of living there, rather than the triumph of ownership, take center stage. When the family finally takes possession, I was a lot happier that they had the house than they were.

The relentless piling up of bitter details is wearing. You begin to wonder: didn't anybody in that family ever enjoy himself? Did no one ever look at the sky and say, "What a great day"? Were there no instances of loving-kindness, courage, or generosity? Poverty and blunted ambition could not by themselves have produced the negative attitude toward existence the main character displays. I found myself resenting the dismal picture Naipaul laboriously lays out and holding it against him.

But some months later, reading the letters he exchanged with his father when he first left Trinidad for England, I began to see what was going on. It's clearly Naipaul's view of Trinidad that we're getting in *Biswas,* not his father's. The contrast between the tone of *Biswas* and that of the letters Naipaul wrote home when he left Trinidad at eighteen is stark. The dreary, uncomfortable life the son attributes to the father springs from Naipaul's need to put the island behind him.

When he writes about his first days away from home he can't get over being called "sir," and being treated with respect by service personnel. Most of all, he loves being on his own. On his first night away, he has a layover in New York: he devours the experience. It's what a writer needs and he knows it and it's heaven. When he wrote *Biswas,* Naipaul had already published three novels; he was on his way to becoming a respected author—educated, cosmopolitan, connected to the right people. His livelihood and reputation now depend on his being in foreign places, places that *are* someplace: New York, Oxford, London. Trinidad by contrast appears as a dead end. Naipaul can't live there: it may have provided him with material for a while, but there's no audience for his work, no people to know, no one to talk to. It's as if he were trying to convince himself that life in Trinidad was a bad deal.

And there's another reason to turn his back on the island. Later, in a book about the people who had most influenced him, I learned that Naipaul's father wanted to be an author, too, not just a journalist, and had published a small book of short stories that never went anywhere. Though Naipaul twice republished his father's collection of stories, hoping to give him a better chance at an audience, neither attempt succeeded. This was the clue. Naipaul identifies with his father and believes his father should have had a chance to become known in the world for his writing in the same way that he, Vidia, had. He owes his father everything—his love of literature, his education, his chance to break free of Trinidad. Guilt that his father never had the opportunities he had, the need to show how circumstance beat his father back time after time, and an equal need to show that Naipaul himself had to stay away at all costs, explain the nature as well as the existence of *Biswas*—the story of why his father didn't make it—with its cornucopia of depressing detail. The concept of success that underlies this rejection of his home is defined in terms of fame, money, prizes, travel, and knowing important people. It has little or nothing to do with family ties, belonging to a community or a nation, connection with a people or a place.

Biswas teaches us to see where Naipaul came from, in his mind: a stagnant economy, few jobs for the educated, uncrossable racial and class lines, a sparse cultural scene. It is an island where for most people there was never enough of anything to go around. On top of that, Vidia experienced the bickering and hierarchy of an extended family, ruled over by a matriarch who tightly controlled the fates of many dependents. There is always a sense of striving against huge odds. Trinidad, in his account of it, shows Vidia the futility of so many things: energy and resources wasted, hopes not coming to fruition, dreams dashed. His description of being in New York that first night away from home is full of the energy of escape—thank God, he'd made it out of there—and an absolute determination to make something of himself. Naipaul is an arrow shot from the bow of his father's defeat.

☾

It was a relief at last to come up with some explanation for the dyspeptic tone of *A House for Mr. Biswas*. But I knew there had to be more to the story than that. Trying to find out about Naipaul by reading *Biswas* had been like pounding my fist on a closed door. The author seemed to give away nothing about himself. But my irritable reaction had less to do with not learning more about Naipaul than with what seemed to me his relentless negativity; as I read, I berated him inwardly for not allowing his characters even one or two moments of unalloyed pleasure. And then I realized that my anger at Naipaul's relentless focus on his father's thwarted existence stemmed partly from the fact that illness had turned my own life into something similar—something that felt pinched and malnourished, blocked. But circumstances had forced me to make peace with it. I was not starting out in life, as Naipaul was, couldn't escape my limitations by traveling abroad and taking on new challenges. My foot was nailed to the floor. I had to find a way to transform the obstacles in my path, or to work my way around them. One way I had of doing that was to read, and in reading this novel I was being put through an endless series of frustrations and discouragements that seemed contrived to shut the door on hope, close down possibilities, and assert the supremacy of adverse circumstance. I'd learned that in getting through the hard places in life it was lethal to maintain a negative mind-set. Refusing promises of hope and redemption was a luxury I couldn't afford.

I'd learned that the bleakness of lost opportunities could be compensated for by embracing the minute chances for happiness that came in the course of daily living: I'd notice how the movement of the thatch palms in the Florida garden, seen out of the corner of the eye, seemed like the motions of a human figure, glimpsed obliquely for a second; or, standing at my kitchen window, I'd take in the tangle of different greens—silver, gray, yellow, blue, emerald, forest—the intersecting shapes and lines of bushes, grasses, and trees, a fantastically complicated tangle against a brilliant blue. I was angry at Naipaul because, for all his keenness of observation, he had failed to see the infinitude of chances one has for appreciating the beauty of the world in the ordinary course of things. I'd started to paint in watercolors as a way of opening up my life, and through painting became more visually attuned to my surroundings. I didn't have to go somewhere else to come into awareness of what was around me. I wasn't able to work, volunteer, go on trips, take courses, or go to parties, but I could— sometimes, when my energy allowed—do a painting, and feel connected to the world that way, by making something. All this lay behind the resistance and irritation I felt as I read *Biswas*. I wanted to say to Naipaul what we used to say to each other as kids: "Wake up and die right."

Much later it occurred to me, rereading these sentences, that Naipaul failed to include even one moment of pure joy in his story because he simply did not remember any such thing. It occurred to me that what I had thought of as his sophomoric refusal either to appreciate or enjoy any aspect of life in Trinidad stemmed not from perverseness but from inability, and that what kept him from ascribing to Mr. Biswas even one happy day was ancient, unremitting, ineradicable pain. And I saw that my own ability to experience joy in the face of privation might be owing to an upbringing much easier and more benign than his.

At the time, I went back to the novel and reread several scenes. Again, their bleakness and meanness penetrated me. But with those impressions came others: for instance, a streak of affection on Naipaul's part for the characters and customs of his youth. Alongside the stream of resentment, criticism, and disgust, there sometimes ran a rivulet of fondness and humor that softened the picture at its edges. One small incident epitomized this feeling. Mr. Biswas's son, Anand (Naipaul's surrogate in the novel), has been living with his father, who's in charge of overseeing the workers on one of his in-laws' plantations, a low-level, unsatisfying job. Anand is playing by himself one day, when he comes across two men who are looking for work squatting in the shade. They're waiting for his father. Pretending to find pennies in the roadside gravel (they've dropped them there themselves)—first one finds a coin, then the other—they trick Anand into digging for coins. Anand hops back forth between them, digging here, digging there, finding a cent.

> "I could keep it?"
> "But is yours," the younger man said. "You find it."

Anand, who has said his father would be by in the truck any minute, now tells them that Biswas is not his father. "He just a man I know." They argue about it. The older man, who is fat, asks for the coins back, grabs Anand, and threatens to hit him. Anand threatens to tell his father, just as his father arrives in the truck.

> "Afternoon, boss," the fat man said.
> "Haul your tail. Who the hell tell you you could lay your hand on my son?"
> "Son, boss?"
> "He try to thief my money," Anand said.
> "Was a game," the fat man said.
> "Haul off!" Mr. Biswas said. "Job! You not looking for any job. You not getting any, either."

They argue, exchange insults, the men back away, and the scene ends with Anand showing his father the pennies he had found: "The road full of money," he says. "They was finding silver. But I didn't find any."

This scene crystallizes the nature of the world Naipaul creates. Its essence is disappointment. Anand doesn't find silver. The men don't get jobs. The father is angry. There are far more disturbing episodes in the novel—bitter family fights involving both parents and children, unhappiness and feuding between Biswas and his wife, all taking place within the grating, competitive, back-biting atmosphere of the extended family. But a humor floats in and out of the scene, a nostalgia for the place and time, a love for the local dialect, that let us feel the pull that childhood and home still exert on Naipaul. They can't make up for the atmosphere of friction, frustration, and defeat, but their presence adds a barely detectable sweetness to the scene that makes it funny and sad as well.

Commentators on *Biswas* use words like "epic" and "masterpiece" to describe the novel, noting Naipaul's "flawless" ear and his skill as a raconteur "keen for irony." It's true, Naipaul is a supreme ironist, and the virtuosity of his writing is beyond dispute. His accomplishment in re-creating the tenor and texture of the Indian subculture on Trinidad is enormous. But for me the main fact of the novel is its feeling of frustrated hopes, softened occasionally by a longing for that world despite its disappointments. Sometimes, when I read it, my throat closes, and I feel the misery underneath. I want to know what, in Naipaul's experience of this place, has caused him so much pain that he cannot write even a single scene that is not shadowed with unhappiness and discontent.

One paragraph in the novel supplies not so much an answer to this question as a clue to where to look. It comes at the end of a brilliant résumé of the ways the children of the extended family alternately deride, adulate, slander, and turn on one another, a passage tinged with Naipaul's signature attitude of detached amusement, and ends with a description of Naipaul himself, in the character of Anand:

> Though no one recognized his strength, Anand was among the strong. His satirical sense kept him aloof. At first this was only a pose, and imitation of his father. But satire led to contempt, and . . .

contempt, quick deep, inclusive, became part of his nature. It led to inadequacies, to self-awareness and a lasting loneliness. But it made him unassailable.

This sudden, not-to-be-repeated dropping of a mine-shaft into the interior of Anand's psyche is tantalizing and revealing. For me, it's evidence that Naipaul has been wounded and is in need of defense. And so he adopts the satirical attitude his father had adopted, knows that his reaction is counterproductive—the price is isolation—yet adopts it anyway. His self-diagnosis is pitiless and precise. He has immured himself securely inside the self-made armor of contempt, put himself in prison and thrown away the key. Impregnability is what he requires, and he is willing to take the consequences. From the reader he does not want an iota of sympathy. What's done is done.

The image of Naipaul as a warrior fortified against all comers by the armor of contempt is a good disguise. So convincing that Naipaul himself believes it. I do not. Contempt, and the rage that accompanies it, comes from pain. The reason Naipaul is so good at observing behaviors that are cruel and self-serving, living conditions that are harsh and demeaning, expressions of frustration that are destructive and out of control, is that he himself felt their effects so keenly. He meticulously catalogues the thousand ways in which life had disappointed Mr. Biswas because he himself has felt them. How could it be that not a single indignity, not one dismissive glance, not the smallest betrayal escaped him, if he had not himself felt their sting? So, yes, the novel does explain his father's failure to be a literary success, and it does justify Naipaul's own decision to stay in England rather than return to Trinidad. It also, and more importantly, constitutes a massive case against the world Naipaul grew up in, fueled by the pain and outrage of someone who had felt victimized by it. The tone of wry amusement and well-controlled irony the narrator adopts is his defense against the suffering and hurt that that world had inflicted on him, a suffering and hurt too deep and too painful to acknowledge. The refusal is adamantine and heroic. For the sake of maintaining his pride, he cuts himself off from love and belonging. He has to see himself as "among the strong," stronger and better than the rest.

After persistent seeking and reflection, I had managed to extract at least this much about Naipaul from *A House for Mr. Biswas.* I hadn't learned as much as I wanted, but I had made a beginning, so I decided to see if I could make some headway with Theroux. I wasn't really sure of what I was doing. I was stumbling along reaching for something, some knowledge, I didn't know quite what, and hoping to come up with it, whatever it might be. The difficulty of the search was part of the attraction. I was disappointed that clues were so scarce and that my ability to interpret them felt limited, but the struggle made it feel worth doing, and I needed something to do.

4

Going Places

By the grace of God our apartment in New York is located around the corner from the Strand Book Store, a book-lover's paradise but hell for someone with ME (chronic fatigue syndrome). The air is dry and full of book dust; it's unbelievably overheated; there's no ventilation; it's crowded; depending on where you are, the light is either glaring or too dim; often you have to walk up and down stairs to find what you're looking for; you could die of dehydration, never mind exhaustion. But I love it, of course. When I went looking for Theroux's most famous book I hadn't yet imposed on myself the never-stay-longer-than-fifteen-minutes rule—and barely made it home without having to sit down on the sidewalk to rest.

I'd been looking forward to reading *The Great Railway Bazaar,* the book that put Theroux on the map for most people, but the Strand didn't have it, so I bought the next best thing, the one he wrote immediately afterward, *The Old Patagonian Express.* A weird book. Almost from the first moment you know there's no point to the journey the author is taking and that he's only going on this trip because he needs something to write about. Since *The Great Railway Bazaar,* a travel book, had been much more successful than any of his novels thus far, he's hoping to hit it big again with a sequel. But there wasn't enough energy in what I was reading to distract me from the question, why are you doing this? If one is being entertained, one doesn't care about the author's motive in writing the book. But I wasn't enjoying what I was reading, and at least one reason for that was that Theroux wasn't enjoying himself either.

He takes a long, arduous journey from Medford, Massachusetts, to Patagonia—by train—which, it turns out, is not the best way to go, but he has to go by train because that's what he did in his last book. Most of the time the experience amounts to nothing more than an extended feat of endurance. Not endurance in the sense of testing your mettle against physical challenges—as in, say, mountain climbing—riding trains through Central and South America is nothing like trying to get to the top of K2—it's just uncomfortable and boring. The trains he rides are dusty, their seats are hard, he shivers with cold, eats bad food, has stomach trouble, talks to people who bore him. When he gets off the train he stays in dingy hotels, encounters poverty and suffering virtually everywhere, not to mention disgusting odors and filth. In most of the places he visits the people are destitute—not just a few people, but the vast majority. In the cities, everywhere he looks there's dirt, disorganization, and despair. Children sleeping in doorways on thin pieces of cardboard, lying on top of each other for warmth. Women selling rotten fruit at the train station. It's hard to be presented with such scenes day after day, station after station. It would be one thing if Theroux were there to chronicle political and social injustice, but he's not. Nor is he there to gather information about how people live in Central and South America. He's not there because he has to get to Patagonia for some practical reason—to visit a sick relative, collect an inheritance, take a job. If he were going there for any of these reasons, he'd have flown. Everyone tells him airplane is the best way to go. No. He's there, by his own account, just for the heck of it. So why does he keep going? Well, we know why. He needs to write a book about it and get paid.

After a while, I didn't mind. I became invested in the idea of his reaching Patagonia just to get there and write about it later. I found myself wanting to know what would turn up at the next stop or over the next border because, little by little, I'd become interested in what he had to say. Oddly, the very pointlessness of his being in any particular place along the route adds to the interest of the journey. Without the pressure of necessity, the basis for making decisions is taken away. He is free to do and see and say whatever he wants. He decides to leave a town on the spur of the moment because there are no good hotels, or because the town is ugly and depressing, or for no reason other than that he's supposed to be going to Patagonia. The motivelessness of his journey gives his actions a weightless quality, as if he were in a kind of existential limbo. Theroux recognizes this the first time he comes to a place where he sees people leading lives comparable to his own—paying electric bills, buying vacuum cleaners, taking their children to school. Because they belong where they are, have responsibilities, a reason for doing what they do, they make him feel superfluous, without a compass. He's more comfortable in towns that represent some extreme of weather or economic deprivation, more at home with people who are abandoned by society or marginalized by their own suffering, because they don't force him to ask why he isn't at home with his own family, and more generally, why he is here on this planet at all. Without acknowledging it explicitly, Theroux confronts the central question of existence: why live? To his credit, he doesn't try to answer it with a formula. He doesn't know the answer. The best he can do is write about his experience along the way.

When I searched for a passage to illustrate the kind of experience Theroux chronicles, it was hard to find one that wasn't too long to quote. His descriptions of the places he passes through are lengthy and highly detailed; the conclusions they reach depend for their force on the specificity and amplitude of the buildup. As scenes unfurl before his eyes hour after hour, the descriptions suffer from the ennui of a long train trip—monotony is the enemy. Theroux brings this to our attention as a feature of the subject matter itself.

> The landscape changed; the villages remained the same. You think: *I've been here before.* The village is small and has a saint's name. The station is a shed, open on three sides, and near it are piles of orange peels and blown-open coconut husks with fibrous hair, and waste paper and bottles. That gray trickle of waste water gathering in a green yellow pool; that woman with a basket on her head . . . the ten filthy children and the small girl with the naked infant on her back . . . the limping dog, the whining pig, the dozing man with his head resting on his left shoulder. . . . It seems so familiar you begin to wonder if you have been traveling in a small circle, leaving in the morning and every day arriving in the heat of the afternoon at this same village . . . the vision of decrepitude repeating like the dream that demands that you return again and again to the same scene. . . . Can it be that after weeks of train travel you have gone no farther than this and have only returned once again to this squalid place?

The plaintiveness in this passage escaped me the first time around. I was struck mainly by the piled-up details and thought that, for all his awareness of the misery they represent, Theroux's take on them is superficial—he's more concerned about his own boredom than anything else. But it's not only the tedium of repetition Theroux finds wearing. The entire experience is hard to take. There's a laboriousness in the long list of particulars, many of which I've omitted, that reflects a kind of battle fatigue on his part. It's as if he has to force himself to note the gray trickle of waste water, the girl with the naked infant, the whining pig—he wants to make us see what he saw, but, even as he adds detail after detail, basically, he's resisting the experience: "Can it be that after weeks of train travel you . . . have only returned once again to this squalid place?" The feeling that this is not what he'd bargained for when he set out arises again and again. As the train pulls out of the little town, he comments: "Because you have seen so many departures like this, the village leaves no impression. . . . But somewhere in the memory, these poor places accumulate, until you pray for something different, a little hope to give them hope. To see a country's poverty is not to see into its heart, but it is very hard to look beyond such pitiable things." He knows that there is more beneath the surfaces he's describing and that he has not seen into the country's heart. But the task of exploring that heart is overwhelming. He begins the next paragraph, "We ascended another range of hills," and we're back to scenery again. It's a relief for the reader as well as for the narrator, but also a disappointment. In the mountains, as in the terrible cities, there is more suffering than can be faced. And more truth in that suffering than can be perceived by a man headed for Patagonia so that he can write about it afterward. Another person might have reacted differently, might have decided that writing travel books was less important than working for social justice, or that the only way to understand the terrible squalor he saw everywhere lay in the realm of spirituality or economic history and would have abandoned his project as a result. Theroux keeps going. He has a family at home to support, a public to satisfy, and a publisher who is waiting for his next book. I saw that his heart had been touched by those cities and villages and that nevertheless he couldn't afford to let that change his course. Finally I understood why he was going to Patagonia: he was doing his best to earn a decent living, and it was an honorable choice. How many times, I wonder, did he wish he could drop the whole thing, go to the nearest airport, and get a plane ticket home? I'd told myself I wanted to know what it was like to be a professional writer and make a living by one's pen. Well, here was the answer. You do what you have to in order to survive. Ann Patchett waited tables, taught, and ground out stories for mass-market publications. Paul Auster lived hand to mouth for years and years. I remembered what Melville had written in one of his famous letters to Hawthorne, complaining of having to meet the demands of the market: "Dollars damn me . . . , and all my books are botches." Theroux was following the advice Naipaul had given him: do anything but teach.

In the end, Theroux gets to Patagonia, but there's no sense of closure, or that a destination of any importance has been reached. The fineness of his observations along the way is indisputable, but his insights and his emotional responses to what he sees seem thin, perhaps because it's not humanly possible to respond adequately to such an enormous onslaught of sensation and feeling: who could process it all, who could make sense of it, who could provide the context necessary to grasp the significance of experiences gleaned from traversing an entire continent?

Whether or not you like this kind of travelogue is a matter of taste and temperament. For me, it offers both too much and not enough: too much information and not enough comprehension. I understand why the book is the way it is. Seen from the perspective of an author struggling to make ends meet, rather than from that of an armchair critic, *The Old Patagonian Express* is a heroic effort. Still, the book didn't seem to have been written by the same person who wrote *Sir Vidia's Shadow*. When I'd told a friend, a fan of Theroux's, that I was about to read it, she said, "Oh, that's the one where he doesn't like any of the places he goes." She had it right. But she'd loved *The Great Railway Bazaar,* so I downloaded it onto my Kindle and off I went. It was fresher, had more energy, and took you to more interesting places, but it was the same thing all over again. There's not enough reflectiveness, not enough self-consciousness. Theroux doesn't see *himself* differently for having been in all those places. He doesn't see himself very much at all. I wanted to meet the man who had been Naipaul's friend and had written about their relationship; he was a deeper person. Maggie, who had given me *Sir Vidia's Shadow* and *A House for Mr. Biswas,* now gave me her copy of *My Other Life,* a semi-fictional memoir Theroux had written two years before *Sir Vidia's Shadow.* There, she said, I might find the person I was looking for, and eventually I did. But first Dogen, and several other books, intervened. One thing led to another.

5

Fame

Most mornings, sitting on the sofa in our apartment near the Strand, I read around in *The Essential Dogen: Writings of the Great Zen Master,* edited by Kazuaki Tanahashi and Peter Levitt. I do it as a way to anchor myself before meditating. The firm cushions of the sofa, the light coming through the windows behind me, the familiar furniture, the book in my hand—these things orient me not just in space but inwardly. One morning, at the end of the chapter on precepts, I read the following passage: "Loving fame is worse than breaking a precept. Breaking a precept is a transgression at a particular time. Loving fame is like an ailment of a lifetime. Do not foolishly hold on to fame, or do not ignorantly accept it. Not to accept fame is continuous practice. To abandon fame is continuous practice."

The paragraph scored a hit. Meditation or no meditation, a desire for fame had been with me ever since I could remember. Power and money—two other unmentionables—I didn't care that much about. But fame!—I didn't know why I wanted it, I just did. In the world I grew up in, ambition and the desire for fame were not ideas one could admit to entertaining consciously. They were socially unacceptable, even immoral. If you had such desires, they had to remain behind the scenes, pulling the strings without anyone's being aware, not even yourself. If you succeeded at something and became famous—voilà!—wonderful. But the success couldn't arise from the desire for recognition (that would be in poor taste); it had to stem from some combination of industry, talent, and accomplishment. So it was some time before I could openly admit to myself that I was ambitious and wanted to be known for something.

On the day I read the passage from Dogen, which forced me to see my desire for fame as a lifelong ailment, the mail brought a copy of Naipaul's 2002 collection of essays, *The Writer and the World.* And who should have written the blurbs on the back cover but Daphne Merkin, whom I revere for her writing on depression, and Vivian Gornick, well-known feminist and author of *Fierce Attachments,* a mother-daughter memoir I admire. Here's what Gornick had to say: "Naipaul brings to the non-fiction genre an extraordinary capacity for making art out of lucid thought." Yes, I said to myself, lucid thought was Naipaul's most distinguished gift. She continues: "His is a way of thinking about the world that will compel our attention throughout his working life and well beyond"—a nod to the ephemerality of fame and a tribute to Naipaul's ability to withstand it. And finally, an all-out affirmation of the surpassing value of his work: "I can no longer imagine a world without Naipaul's writing." There's fame for you. And then, stoking the fires of envy even further, there was the secondary fame of those who testified for Naipaul: Merkin and Gornick.

All at once it came to me that my attitude toward both Theroux and Naipaul was tainted; it consisted of more than admiration, curiosity, and a strong sense of rapport. I was attracted to them because they were famous. I was trying to get to know them better not just because I was interested in them for themselves, but because at some level I must have felt that if I spent time with their work, some of their glamour and acclaim might rub off on me. And it also occurred to me that I might have wished to find fault with them and unconsciously enjoyed picking them apart so that I could prove to myself that their fame did not make them better than I was, since, though they might be outstanding as writers, as human beings they had a lot to answer for. Could it be that on the surface I was ready to praise them but that underneath was a crouching tiger ready to spring, ready to drag them down so that I could feel better about myself? The desire for fame is envy's first cousin.

In the passage from Dogen, there's no reason given for why wanting fame is bad, so I try to answer the question on my own. In my case, I thought, the desire for fame stems from wanting to be endorsed by others, to be legitimized, respected, admired, and, most of all, loved; it comes also from wanting to feel valued and important, wanting to exist more fully by virtue of being the object of other people's attention. It's sort of like wanting a hairpiece because you're short on hair: you don't have enough to start out with so you try to supply yourself with it artificially. I recognize that this existential need can never be met by having fame, but knowing this makes no difference.

For a while, I was well enough known in my profession to have received a certain amount of attention. I was invited to give lectures at colleges and universities around the country, speak at conferences, do radio interviews. This was something I enjoyed. It made me feel good for two reasons. One was simple ego gratification. These people had chosen *me* to give the commencement address, talk to the freshman class, keynote their conference. I felt rewarded for the effort I'd put into my writing by being at the center of attention for a few days. The other reason for feeling gratified was, the invitations indicated that my work was having an impact—at least I hoped that that was what it meant. I believed that the world would be a better place if my ideas took root and flourished. But whatever effect my ideas may have had, over time I discovered in conversations with members of the audience after my talks that there were ways in which my relationship to the people I met was skewed.

In some cases, I noticed, I became a blank screen onto which people projected their desires, hatreds, needs for justification, and pet peeves. Faculty members and students used my presence to bolster their own position in the department, or as an excuse to air institutional grievances and long-standing resentments. I saw that being "known" could be an imaginary relationship on both sides. You imagine that they're captivated by your ideas, and they imagine that you're fulfilling some need of their own. It's disconcerting to find out that, often as not, neither is true. What you came there for—to offer people your views, and in so doing, to produce a change in them—seems a distant and unrealistic goal. Emotionally, for a while, the spotlight can provide you with a rush, a surge of happiness and well-being, a sense of being larger and more powerful than you usually feel. But it doesn't last. One minute it feels great, and the next minute you're left with your same old uninspired, put-one-foot-in-front-of-the-other self. My husband, who is a lot more famous than I'll ever be, would call me from time to time from some place where he'd been lecturing and tell me he felt almost ashamed or sickened after all the adulation he'd received. That's the crash.

When I find myself envying famous people, the ones I envy most are those who never lost the chance life gave them to do something that mattered. They had grabbed the opportunity, taken the risk, put forth the effort, and been rewarded by seeing the difference their efforts had made in the world. I wanted to be like that, a person who had striven toward a goal and achieved it, preferably for the benefit of the whole human race! The idea was to be famous oneself, yes, but only because of what one was doing for others. The notion that there were people who worked obscurely their whole lives for high ideals and went to their graves unsung filled me with sorrow and bitterness. I know the belief that nothing is worth doing unless others recognize it is the epitome of false values. If recognition itself is the goal, then the work is empty. But it wasn't that simple. I wanted to do good, to feel that I had done good, *and* to know that my work had been recognized.

Then one day it occurred to me to ask myself what I had done that I considered truly worthwhile, and then to ask if I cared whether or not other people knew about it. The first thing that came to mind was the seven months I spent interning as a hospital chaplain in Chicago, visiting people in their hospital rooms and in the Emergency Room, spending time with patients in the Intensive Care Unit, attending the bedsides of the dying and talking with their families. This work connected me to life like nothing else I'd ever done, and it never occurred to me to think about whether other people knew about it. The two things—being deeply connected to life and other people's ideas about me—seemed completely unrelated.

Then another moment came to mind. I'm riding in the back of an open truck with kids from a camp in Maine where I'm a counselor. We're on the way home from swimming in the ocean. Energized from having been in the icy water, feeling the air rush by my face, being with the children, who were in good spirits, and knowing they were all right, I felt alive and complete. As for getting some kind of credit for it, the idea never crossed my mind. I had never put these experiences together with my craving for renown. The fact was, at the deepest level, I didn't crave it at all.

I think, now, that more than fame, it's communication I want: being known by other people, to be in contact with them somehow. But where does this desire come from? Why is this what I want? The same question can be put to anyone who writes, especially to people like Naipaul and Theroux, who have made writing the center of their lives. In reading their books I was trying to discover, among other things, what made them want to be writers. In searching for an answer to this question I was looking for a piece of myself.

At the beginning of *The Scarlet Letter,* in the Custom-House essay, Hawthorne famously talks about his relation to his audience. Playing cat and mouse with his readers, somewhat coyly, as always, Hawthorne nevertheless lets us see what's driving him: namely, the need to speak truthfully to unknown others who are of like mind, who can receive his words more fully, perhaps, than those who are closest to him: "When he casts his leaves forth upon the wind, the author addresses, not the many who will fling aside his volume, or never take it up, but the few who will understand him, better than most of his school mates or his life-mates." He is looking for a kindred spirit, or spirits, whose minds are uniquely attuned to his own. He goes further: "Some authors, indeed . . . indulge themselves in such confidential depths of revelation as could fittingly be addressed, only and exclusively, to the one heart and mind of perfect sympathy; as if the printed book, thrown at large upon the world, were certain to find out the divided segment of the writer's own nature, and complete his circle of existence by bringing him into communion with it."

This has always seemed to me a perfect expression of the desire that motivates writing, at least on the part of shy, introverted people who, unwilling to risk exposing themselves to others face to face, nevertheless want to be known by them. Having gone this far, Hawthorne, ever cautious, backs off several paces, distancing himself from those who would speak "all," and assuring us that, though he will reveal himself to us, he will still keep "the inmost Me behind its veil." I'm convinced that the backing and filling is all cover. What he wants is that divided segment of his own nature, the one soul that is the perfect twin of his own who can complete him. If he leaves room for doubt as to whether this is really his aim, it's not because he's ashamed of it, but because he fears it might not be possible to achieve. He is shielding himself from disappointment. A spiritual advisor once told me that the highest form of communication is communion. Hawthorne wants communion.

If someone asked me why I write, that would be my answer, too, the desire to be known. This is a spiritual need, a longing as deep as any that we have. To be known is to have one's existence validated, to be affirmed in our very being, simply by being seen. In some circumstances, our emotional survival depends on our having a witness who will listen to us; it is all that we need, and without it, we cannot survive.

Seeking communion with strangers through the medium of the printed word might not seem to be the most direct way of achieving the intimacy that communion implies. Why not open your heart to the people you're closest to? Why not know and be known by them face to face? Hawthorne thought his schoolmates and lifemates might not understand him, and perhaps he was right. One of the experiences we don't have very often while we're growing up is the experience of being listened to sympathetically and with an open heart when trying to give voice to something of great importance to us. Genuine openness, sharing one's inner feelings and thoughts with parents, children, siblings, and even friends, has to be learned through experience, example, encouragement, and practice. It's not automatic. If one is listened to sympathetically and without judgment at an early age, the habit of intimacy can be learned, and if it's not learned then, can take some time and effort to acquire.

One day a year or two ago I was on the phone with my cousin's wife, J., who started telling me about visits she and my cousin had made to my parents years before. On every one of these visits, she said, there came a time when my parents would launch into long encomiums of me, singing my praises, going on and on about my accomplishments and how well I was doing. My cousins would roll their eyes inwardly and wait it out.

The story made me extremely uncomfortable, not only because of what my cousins had had to sit through, but also because of the view it gave me of the role I'd played in my parents' lives. My parents had let me know in a thousand ways that I was loved; they'd made me feel safe and cared for, a state of affairs that, for a child, is priceless and irreplaceable. But I'd had no idea that my achievements had meant so much to them. I wish they had told me. Having worked so hard to perform at peak capacity, whatever I was doing, I would have liked to have known that my efforts had produced the very results I'd been aiming for. The conversation revealed something else as well. While I'm sure that my parents' joy in my success was genuine, it was also clear that, in a not so subtle way, they had used my accomplishments to reflect glory on themselves. On the surface their boasting was about me, but underneath it was intended as proof of their own success. My parents loved me *and* they needed to see themselves validated. They had their own desires to be seen as worthy and accomplished, so they used my achievements as currency. It was natural. I could understand it. But it took me aback nevertheless. I didn't want to be a star in their crown. I wanted to be loved and understood, which wasn't the same thing. About a year later, a cousin on the *other* side of my family told me that he had, more than once, been subjected to the same experience, being bombarded by my parents with praises of me; when I said I'd known nothing about it, he was amazed.

Wanting to be recognized as successful by the members of one's own family, whether one is a child or a parent, is a mini-version of the wish to be famous. Perhaps it's the origin of that wish. How many people grow up filled with the conviction that they're so lovable exactly as they are that there's no need for them to demonstrate their worthiness in any external form, no need to perform or achieve because they're already okay? Not very many, I would guess. There's a story that my friend and mentor Parker

Palmer tells on himself in this regard that comforts me. I tell it because Parker is one of the kindest, warmest, most intelligent, and most highly developed human beings I've ever known. It's from the chapter entitled "When Way Closes" in his book *Let Your Life Speak.* At the time he's writing about, Parker was curriculum director at Pendle Hill, a Quaker retreat center in Pennsylvania. He'd been there for about ten years and was ready for a career change. An ad for the presidency of a nearby college caught his eye, and he was in a quandary about whether it was something he should pursue. Unable to make up his mind, he took advantage of a traditional Quaker practice of discernment called a clearness committee, based on the belief that within each of us there's an inner teacher that knows the right direction. The clearness committee—a group of five or six trusted people—spends three hours simply asking questions of the person who's trying to make a critical decision, with the aim of clearing away whatever is blocking that person's ability to discern his or her truth. A small number of procedural rules makes the process both safe and effective. In the case at hand, Parker learned that nothing involved in actually carrying out the responsibilities of the position in question had any appeal for him, and that, without realizing it, what he'd really had in mind when he read the ad was seeing his own picture in the paper and underneath it his name, followed by the words "College President."

If a great soul like Parker, wise, deep, and spiritually attuned, was once gripped by the longing to have his picture in the paper, then maybe my own desire for recognition wasn't so bad after all.

6

A Dancing Dwarf

I'd struck out with Theroux's first travel books—he wasn't really in them—so I decided to go back to Naipaul. I'd get in at the beginning, read his very first novel, *Miguel Street,* and that way discover what made Naipaul tick. I'd tried this once before and it had worked. I'd written my dissertation on Melville's prose style, which changes dramatically three times over the course of his career, and had read everything Melville ever wrote (except the poetry), starting with feature articles he wrote as a young man for the *Lansingburgh Advertiser.* This gave me insight into his early stylistic habits, which tended toward exhibitionism and embroidery, something I wouldn't have known if I'd started with his first novel, whose sentences are symmetrical and orderly. I thought I might make a similar discovery with Naipaul. But no luck. *Miguel Street* is revealing primarily in its refusal to give anything away about the author. But although *Miguel Street* gave me almost nothing that I wanted—there was one thing, at the very end—I had to admit it was a masterpiece.

Miguel Street, published in 1959, is so contemporary in feel and so accomplished it's hard to believe it was a first novel. Naipaul, fresh out of Oxford, where he'd gone at eighteen on a government scholarship, a novice, struggling, wrote it while living in London with a cousin who helped to support them both by doing manual labor. Naipaul's choice of subject is genius. He sketches, one by one, the characters who populated the street where he lived while growing up in Port of Spain; it's exotic—educated first-world readers won't be familiar with everyday life among Indian immigrants in the Caribbean—and the point of view, that of a child growing into adolescence, is perfect: though the lives Naipaul chronicles are full of pain and sadness, they don't seem so because of the fresh matter-of-factness of the boy's perspective.

The book is remarkable for its fanatical clinging to surfaces: surface, surface, and more surface; everything in the book is surface. The stories the young narrator tells confound expectations: they do not have happy endings, they do not exemplify ideas, they do not make a play for our sympathies, and they are careful not to explain themselves in any way. By refusing to follow expected patterns of cause and effect, or to draw familiar morals, they stubbornly avoid reinforcing our desire for human lives to have shape and meaning. Despite their dark content, the sketches have a lightness about them that is wonderful, as if it were a form of play for the narrator to be telling us such tales.

Bogart, named for the movie actor, is liked by everyone, though he always seems bored and superior. A tailor by trade, though he's never been seen making a suit, he sits all day in his room playing solitaire. "What happening there, man?" he'd say when the boy came calling, and then fall silent. In spite of being uncommunicative, Bogart occupies a firm position in the group of men and boys who form the Greek chorus of Miguel Street. But one morning when Hat, the group leader, calls out, as he does every day, "What happening there, Bogart?" there's no reply. Bogart has disappeared. No fuss is made about this. After a while, the men start using his old room for playing cards. A long time later, Bogart turns up and resumes his old habits. His story, told deadpan, by the narrator, is that he'd gone on a ship to British Guiana, deserted, become a cowboy in Venezuela, smuggled goods into Brazil, took girls from Brazil and opened a brothel in Georgetown, where he was arrested even though he'd bribed the police. Now, the men on the street are in awe of him, until one day he disappears again. This time when he returns, having acquired American mannerisms, he's more aggressive. He gives money and chocolate to children, and throws them a big party with lots of Coca-Cola. Bogart leaves a third time, and when he returns, he's arrested. Hat tells the backstory: The first time Bogart showed up after disappearing, he'd left a wife who couldn't have a baby. The last time, he'd gotten a girl pregnant and left her. There is no commentary on this, only a question that ends the chapter: "'But why he leave she?' Eddoes asked." And Hat replies, "To be a man, among we men."

The society of men that forms the background to these sketches provides each member with an identity and a role; belonging to it means that one has a part to play in the ongoing drama of the street. Bogart, it appears, prefers the relative stability and low demand of the group to the risks and responsibilities of family life; being a man in this context seems to mean freedom from women and children. Whatever the case, there's no indication that the author knows or cares that we don't know what to think. The stories in *Miguel Street* are all like this. We're given a string of facts—what happened, who said what to whom, what people thought about it, and what happened afterward. The tone is matter-of-fact, almost nonchalant. No editorializing, no analysis. No one in the novel is taking responsibility for interpreting what occurs, for finding meaning or making judgments. Things just seem to happen one after the other without any sense of causality behind them. The narrator just happens to be on the spot, reporting what he sees and remembers. He doesn't become philosophical or moralistic, he doesn't deliver commentary, because he's only ten or twelve years old. That's the beauty of the preteen perspective. And on account of this, we can relax. We don't have to take the world's problems on our shoulders either. We're off the hook. Sort of.

In contrast to the airiness of tone, the spectacle that we're invited to assist at is no bedtime story. Like Bogart's, most of the stories told here veer between a life of idleness, or purposeless puttering, and sudden spurts of violent activity that don't end well, and usually involve women. Popo, the carpenter, a gentle man, busies himself happily in his shop making "the thing that has no name," while his wife tends to the cows and does all the work. When she leaves him for another man, the men of the street gather in Popo's shop and try to make him feel better. He starts drinking and crying and wanting to beat people up. "Hat said, 'We was wrong about Popo. He is a man like any of we.'" But Popo isn't happy. One day he springs to life, finds the man who took his wife, beats him up, goes home, paints his house red, and furnishes it with stolen furniture. His wife comes back, and Popo is happy. He returns to his old ways, making "the thing without a name." After a while the authorities catch up with him, and though he goes to jail for theft, he comes home a hero—the men of the street respect him even more now. Now—all business—he makes Morris chairs, tables, and wardrobes. But the narrator is sad. He liked the old Popo, who made the thing without a name.

You could say there's a moral here—something to do with becoming socialized, responsible, and how that process drums out the dreamer in us, provokes the gentle soul to violence, turns the experimenter into a hack. But the way the facts are given discourages such conclusions. Things happen; sometimes they turn out well, sometimes not.

George, who has no friends, beats his wife and children and sits on his stoop doing nothing. He buys two Alsatians who terrify the neighbors. When the narrator walks by, George calls him "horseface," and worse, "short-arse": "But how it have people so short-arse in the world?" When George's wife dies—from being beaten, it is said—he sells all the cows (Hat makes a profit on the deal) and continues to beat his children. Elias, the educated, high-minded son, forgives him. But when George turns their house into a brothel for American soldiers, Elias withdraws. And when George marries his fat and giggly (though much-beaten) daughter, Dolly, to a man whose name is Razor for good reason, the son leaves home. Dolly cries at her wedding and disappears. The brothel fails. George dies. And the men of the street collect money for his funeral. There is pathos here, though none is ever expressed. It arises from a rehearsal of the facts alone: the loyal son who finally deserts, the abused daughter who cries at her own wedding, the solidarity of the men who see to it that George gets a proper burial.

What is this, then? Is it local color? Is it some kind of hard-nosed, face-the-facts account of human existence? We are definitely in the modernist era here. First, the narrative is not continuous or complete. The sketchiness of the sketches, the abrupt transitions and randomness of detail imply not only that the narrator is just a boy who can't be expected to know much, but also that there's no guiding hand behind the unfolding of events in general—no God, certainly—and no possibility, ever, of knowing everything, or even of knowing anything very much. And that which we do know is not reassuring. The people being written about are poor; they lead haphazard lives, unprotected by money or influence, subject to sudden disruptions, accidents, bad luck, and their own passions. The stories have a kind of protodocumentary quality, and the hand that selects them seems partial to broken dreams, futile efforts, and repeated disappointments. Only the narrator's youthfulness keeps him from being discouraged by what he sees; at the end he remains hopeful because he's still too young for his own dreams to have been shattered.

As I read on, I began to wonder what the author's attitude toward his material was. He keeps his view closely guarded, hiding behind his youthful stand-in, using him to keep the people whose lives he's describing at a distance—from himself and from us.

We're allowed to sympathize with them, but only up to a point. Under the surface, there's a tug-of-war going on. On the one hand, there's Naipaul's love for his characters—the carpenter who spends years building the thing that has no name, the cart driver who delights in collecting useless junk, the self-taught mechanic who loves to dismantle car engines that, until he gets his hands on them, run perfectly. On the other hand, there's Naipaul's modernist sensibility (if that is what it is), which forbids the direct expression of feeling. He seems to have schooled himself to reproduce something like the impassive stoicism of Hemingway's "Indian Camp," the opening story of *In Our Time,* in which an Indian slits his own throat after watching his wife give birth to a child in agony. Another version of James Joyce's artist standing aside from the human condition paring his fingernails. Or possibly it's the upper-class British horror of emotional display that's motivating him. Whichever it is, Naipaul's affection for his characters pulls against the demands of his sedulously maintained detachment: his love for them comes through most of all in the way he reproduces the native dialect. And this, I think, is the point. The tension between the hard lives of the characters, their failure to flourish and prosper, and the repressed fondness one senses as the moving force of the narrative, is what makes the novel work.

At first, and throughout, the focus is on the people of Miguel Street and their vicissitudes; it hardly ever turns to the boy who tells the stories. We know little of him. But we do know that he is no longer living on Miguel Street. We know he has escaped, and we know, from the way he talks, that he doesn't think of himself as on a par with the characters about whom he's writing. If anything, his primary identification is with us, the readers, for whom these stories are being spun, and this puts him at odds with his subjects, who come from another class, are without education, have not been away from Trinidad, and will never read his book. So what is Naipaul's relationship to these people? Sometimes as I read I was reminded of books of photographs in which the subjects are shown in their native habitat, wearing their clothes and jewelry, seated amid their furniture and possessions, almost like animals in the wild, although in the case of animal photographs, the viewer's superiority to the subject is not always implied. Naipaul has not intended to fall into this trap—the trap of patronage and condescension—but I don't think he avoids it completely.

Having read *Sir Vidia's Shadow,* I know Naipaul is in the habit of referring to people below himself in social status as "infies," short for "inferiors," and that he often treats them accordingly, which is to say, dismissively and at times cruelly—think "bananas and bongos." But *Miguel Street* was composed long before Theroux met Naipaul, so it's possible Naipaul hadn't yet formed these dismissive attitudes. Still. Are these people beloved figures from Vidia's childhood? Or are they just "material"? And what is the sense of life they convey? What does Naipaul suppose his depictions of them are telling us? The answer to that question, if it can be found, lies in the shadow world outside the stories themselves, in the place from which the subjects are being viewed. That place is definitely not Trinidad. It belongs to a different culture, a different mode of life, a different set of assumptions about the world. The series of failures the stories depict—failure to sustain relationships, make a decent living, treat other people with dignity and respect, refrain from violence and drunkenness—imply their opposite: a world glimpsed once or twice in the shadowy figure of a uniformed servant in a house in a well-to-do part of town, a nice house, with a garden and a handsome automobile in the driveway, implying stability, security, a well-ordered life—these things, which, as I say, are barely glimpsed, nevertheless haunt the ramshackle neighborhood in the foreground with its odd assortment of characters. In fact, it's only from the vantage of this other, unseen, existence that the stories about Popo and Bogart and the sadistic George are worth taking so much trouble to tell.

Those outward symbols of a successful bourgeois life stand in for the world from which all these events are being viewed, and this world, the world inhabited by the author—the world of Europe, the United States, and above all England, so far away, so exalted, and unreachable—is the touchstone and benchmark of all earthly doings, the world within which meanings are made. So the fulcrum on which these stories teeter back and forth is the point where the author's divided loyalties balance each other out. Much as he treasures these memories of his native country, in the end Naipaul does not, and cannot, give his whole heart to his childhood companions on Miguel Street. He has not quite granted them full status as human beings. He has withheld from them, if not his deepest affection, then his greatest admiration, because he himself has opted for a different life and cannot help but see his old friends from the perspective he has acquired since leaving them. He has chosen the first world of Western culture over the third world of a British colony. He pays his debt to that world right away, in his first novel, but he withholds himself from it.

It is an act simultaneously of generosity and stinginess. The generosity lies in the artistry with which he does his work. This book is so finely crafted it's hard to praise it enough. The coolness and delicacy with which he selects his incidents, the way he paces each sketch, the use of repetition, the austerity with which he treats his characters, the reluctance to analyze or second-guess— the artfulness with which he times the disclosure of facts, his handling of the local dialect, the subtle weaving together of random details into a single fabric—you'd think he'd been at it for decades. The labor expended on this manuscript is infinite. But at the same time Naipaul is holding back. Although you can feel the author's sympathy and affection for someone like Popo, he never lets us see Popo or anyone he writes about as someone to admire or emulate; he does not present these men as, in any sense, his equals. Their dramas are small-scale: poignant, perhaps, but lacking in significance. There is nothing to look up to here: no acts of courage or daring, no instances of human ingenuity or imagination, piety or humility, almost no tenderness and not too much kindness. One could say that this is because Naipaul, a modernist, a realist, and a secularist, has a vision of human existence that does not include the realm of the ideal or the transcendent; one could say also that he believes that if one feels too much, expresses too much, it will cheapen the emotion, since the value of a writer, in this view, lies in his refusal to distort his material through the expression of feeling. One could say this but it would not alter the fact that *Miguel Street* leaves the depths of human existence unplumbed. Heights and depths of feeling, the visionary and the prophetic, are not in Naipaul's portfolio, at least not yet. And if they are, his diffidence, his caginess, his unwillingness to show his hand when push comes to shove, keep us from knowing anything about them.

If there was ever a book that deflected attention away from its author in a human sense, that book is *Miguel Street.* A perfect artifact of fiction writing, it has a hard enamel coating, shiny and impermeable. Not only do we learn nothing about the author from it, we learn nothing about the first-person narrator, either. Nor do we learn much, if anything, about the interior lives of the characters. All interiority has to be deduced from the surface, and the surface, in most cases, intentionally hides it. Attention is distributed equally among a large number of characters, and, while some are more sympathetic than others, we are not allowed to get too close to any of them. As a text to mine for clues about the kind of person Naipaul is, it's hopeless. But in the search for evidence, a negative, while not as good as a positive, is not nothing. Naipaul does not wish to be intimate with his audience. He does not want to be known by us. His writing is at once a superb display of intelligence and craft, and a long game of hiding.

There is, however, one small exception to Naipaul's rule of not giving himself away. At the very last moment of *Miguel Street,* the young narrator, who, with the help of his mother's bribe to an official, has won a scholarship to go to England, describes his departure from the island in terms that hint at the intensity of his feelings—through understatement, of course—and then leaves us with a phrase that sums up concisely his image of himself at the time, and—who knows?—perhaps forever. He, his mother, and his Uncle Bhakcu, the car repairer, are at the airport.

> The announcement came, a cold, casual thing.
> I embraced my mother.
> I said to Bhakcu, "Uncle Bhak, I didn't want to tell you before, but I think I hear your tappet knocking."
> His eyes shone.
> I left them all and walked briskly towards the aeroplane, not looking back, looking only at my shadow before me, a dancing dwarf on the tarmac.

Writing more deft and succinct than this is hard to come by. Naipaul lets us know how charged and momentous the occasion is for him by noting that the announcement of his plane seemed (by implied contrast) cold and casual. No words could express what he feels when he embraces his mother, so he supplies none. He conveys his affection for Uncle Bhakcu in his remark about the tappet; by his uncle's eyes we know the gift has had its intended effect. For the reader he leaves this final image:

> I left them all and walked briskly towards the aeroplane, not looking back, looking only at my shadow before me, a dancing dwarf on the tarmac.

The image is genius. Naipaul is short. And we know from his response when George called him "short-arse" that the narrator of *Miguel Street* was short and hated it. In the jumping shadow, the narrator, leaving Trinidad to go to Oxford as Naipaul did, sees himself as a dancing dwarf, implying at one and the same time, creative energy and the pain of being misshapen, a freak cavorting in a sideshow. The final scene of the novel contains in condensed, encrypted form the elements that have been repressed throughout: the presence of strong emotion, of the female and familial, and the image of a small creature writhing in agony under the sun. Meanwhile, the cool consciousness that registers them all proceeds to get on a plane without looking back. Who knows what Naipaul had in mind when he came up with this conclusion, what he meant by the dancing dwarf? I doubt that when Theroux titled his book about their friendship he had this image in mind. But it is Sir Vidia's shadow.

7

Archaeology

The dancing dwarf was only a snapshot, but it had possibilities. In *Miguel Street* I'd been looking for evidence of trauma—something to explain the bitterness Naipaul infused into *Biswas*, an etiology of suffering, the equivalent of what Maggie was writing about in her novel: a father coming home loaded for bear, beatings, rages, a mother's heartbreaking slide into alcoholism, daughters who hid from the world the shame of what happened at home. I had learned from Maggie something about the ineluctability of the past, and the importance of turning to face it. Other than the grotesque image of a jumping shadow, I hadn't found anything to work with in Naipaul's first novel, but the search brought to the surface a piece of information from my own past that I had never looked at closely. It's the story I sometimes use to explain to myself emotional problems that otherwise I have no way of accounting for.

I had what appears to have been a happy childhood—parents who doted on me (I was an only child), friends, a good education, opportunities. Nevertheless, I've spent a great many hours over the course of my life in therapists' offices. Feelings of guilt and unworthiness, constant self-criticism, fear of rejection and abandonment: that was my lineup. One diagnosis was chronic anxiety, another, attachment disorder. But why?

The closest I ever came to an answer was this. One evening my husband and I were at a restaurant with my parents and some friends, one of whom, Bob Levy, was an anthropologist who had practiced psychoanalysis earlier in his career. My mother, who was sitting next to Bob, started to tell him about a near-death experience she'd had just after I was born. I was surprised, almost shocked. I was fifty-eight years old and had never heard anything about this before; it felt strange learning about it accidentally by overhearing it at dinner in a restaurant. If I hadn't been sitting where I was, I would never have heard it at all. After I was born, my mother had contracted puerperal fever, also called childbed fever, in the days before penicillin, when eight out of ten women who got it died. She had escaped, but barely. She described the calm she had felt as she left her body, and the complete absence of fear. When Bob asked her, twice, if she'd felt any regret at leaving an infant behind, she said no. But that was not what had gotten my attention as much as the fact, which then emerged, that my mother had spent six weeks in the hospital recovering from her illness, and that I, too, had been in the hospital all that time, though not with her. It was news to me.

Strangely, years before, I'd taken it into my head to volunteer for a program at the university hospital near where I lived in which volunteers would come in and hold babies who had to be there for extended periods. Research had shown that infants in their earliest days needed to be held and talked to, rocked and soothed, in order to develop properly. But the ponderous procedures turned me off—meetings in stately conference rooms, a large, heavy binder full of information, forms to fill out, several preparatory sessions; in relation to the act of cuddling babies it all seemed impossibly cumbersome and bureaucratic. I dropped out. But what intuition had led me to that particular form of service? Though I had no conscious knowledge of it at the time, was it that I'd spent the first six weeks of my life alone in a hospital? At around the same period, I'd been volunteering at a homeless shelter. Was that, too, a result of an unconscious urge to mother my former self?

Many times I've tried to picture what those six weeks must have been like: a large, square room, fluorescently lit and predominantly white, filled with cribs. I'm lying in one of them, waiting for someone to come and pick me up. From time to time a nurse comes to feed me; at intervals, someone changes my diaper; once a day I am washed. Was that all? Did anyone come to see me? Did my father, after work, after he'd spent time with my mother, come to the room where I was and ask if I could be held? I had two aunts in the city; did they ever come to pick me up? What was it like for an infant to be lying there alone twenty-four hours a day, day after day? No one had ever said a word to me about this my entire life. My mother herself had told me more than once about having been very sick, had described to me the beautiful Italian nurse named Iris who had been so kind, who had sung to her when she lay there motionless, unable to move even a pinky finger. When my mother told me these things, I was enthralled, but too young to have wondered about where I'd been when this was happening.

From this narrative I've eked out an explanation for issues that have dogged me much of my life: a feeling that the world belonged to other people but not to me, a conviction that I was somehow cut off from normal experience, a fear of being left out or left behind to fend for myself. It's taken me ages to learn that I'm not different from everybody else, that my experience is not anomalous, that I'm in no way a pariah. And after a lifetime of impatience I've learned that waiting is not necessarily the worst thing in the world, though I'm still easily discouraged. Was that hospital stay—featureless, impersonal, boring to the point of annihilation—was that how these and other problems began? Six weeks is a long time for an infant. An eternity. On the basis of that experience, my image of the world and of myself must have been at least partly formed. What effects it had and may still be having I've yet to fully understand, but thanks to Maggie, and to Naipaul, it's there now and available for questioning.

Having arrived at this point, I wanted to piece together a similar explanation for issues which, I could tell from the tone of *Biswas,* had dogged Naipaul all his life. I knew from *Biswas* that Naipaul's father was mentally unstable. He didn't drink or beat his wife, but his behavior at times was peculiar. There were family fights, shouting, pushing, and the endless jockeying for position that constituted life in the extended family. Naipaul's mother and her sisters were members of a hierarchy ruled over by their mother, the matriarch, who controlled everything. Naipaul's mother seems to have been a strong, confident person, sure of her opinions and of her place in the scheme of things. His father, an outsider, a financial dependent and social inferior, was in a weak position vis-à-vis his wife and her powerful relations. Naipaul, who had four sisters, one older than he, and a younger brother, was the oldest male. There was the violence and misogyny of the men who populated his street when he was growing up in Port of Spain. Whether any of this adds up to trauma isn't clear; certainly the materials are there. One day at the French bakery in Boca Raton, I got Maggie to tell me her theory of what had happened to Naipaul. Her ideas grew out of her years of psychotherapy, readings in psychology, and her long struggle to understand her father, who had been rejected by his mother at the age of two, and whose arsenal of aggressive-defensive behavior, directed against his wife and children, included a blistering contempt. The Freudian concepts of early trauma and child development that she laid out were more complex than I'd realized, but in order to understand Naipaul's formation—and my own—I needed to understand them.

A child has to be a certain age, Maggie said, before it's possible for her to form conscious memories. But even the experiences she can't recall will settle in some form in the unconscious mind and be retrievable in the form of feelings associated with them, though there's no memory of the events as such. So although I can't recall my first six weeks of life, feelings of having been physically and emotionally abandoned will likely be with me in some form forever.

She went on. An infant's separation from his primary caregiver occurs over time as the child matures and is lovingly supported. But if, during this process, the toddler experiences some trauma in relation to his mother—a perceived loss of her affection or violence—the trauma can result in feelings of dual misery: a lifelong feeling of dependency on his mother (since his dependency needs weren't properly met) and a lifelong anger toward her (because she hurt him). As a consequence, the early, disappointing mother is found again in all women the grown man encounters. He'll have contempt for women, of course (because they are all his mother and he is longing to separate from her), and may become a womanizer, a "user" of women, to prove to himself that women mean nothing to him and that he's not dependent on them.

Maggie reasoned that something like this must have happened to Naipaul. He must have received a wound in relation to his mother at an early age that set going the process I've just described. Since his mother belonged to a powerful family, the separation was doubly hard because, as a male, he was forced to identify with his father, whose status in the family was low. As Naipaul matured, he adopted his father's defense against the world—contempt—which later blossomed into a well-developed misogyny, and meanness to those he considered below him. Though sketchy and based largely on extrapolation, this view does account for a lot of Naipaul's behavior as an adult, more of which I became aware of later on.

In piecing together a rationale for the kind of person Naipaul turned out to be, thinking always that he was completely different from me, I began uneasily to see certain similarities. I, too, had an inherited streak of contempt. When my mother wanted to lash out, which wasn't often, contempt was her chief weapon. There was a story she liked to tell about being at a family party where a man was making derogatory remarks about Jews. Though my mother's family was Catholic, she herself had abandoned the church. After this man had made a particularly offensive comment, my mother cut in and said in an imperious tone: "Spoken like a true Christian." I can still hear her cutting tone of voice, the imperiousness, the sneer. She told the story with pride, repeatedly, and each time I was proud when I heard it, impressed by her courage, her cleverness, and her moral righteousness. I didn't see its similarity to the contempt she sometimes wielded against me. And I didn't see how I had picked it up and added it to my own repertoire of defenses, imitating her tone of voice and assumption of superiority, until one day in a psychiatrist's office, the therapist asked, after something I'd said, "Whose voice is that?" To my dismay, I recognized it as my mother's voice, and later realized that I frequently used it against myself. The contemptuous introject was a stalwart member of my inner cast of characters, but it existed for the most part below the level of observation. Naipaul, too, I imagine, used this voice against himself, without being aware of it, just as I did.

Contempt strikes me as a defense latched onto by people who suspect they are not as good as others, a forceful way to fight back against what they fear may be true. One grasps at it, relishing its effects—feeling strong, superior, and self-satisfied—in order to compensate for the intolerable alternative—inferiority and helplessness, the dancing dwarf. Naipaul believed, as he tells us in *Biswas,* that brandishing the weapon of contempt made him unassailable. I would say, it made him feel that way, temporarily. He reached for it in order to survive growing up amid the fractiousness of his mother's family. Later, when he got to England

and discovered that he was the wrong race, the wrong class, the wrong color, the wrong height, and may have spoken, at first, with the wrong accent, it must have become even more indispensable.

Some people would say that digging up bits of history in order to explain one's own or other people's behavior is self-serving and a waste of time. That is not how I see it. This is the archaeology of being human: digging into the past for answers to the puzzle of the present. The artifacts can be fragmentary, mysterious, and sometimes, as in the stories told above, uncannily interrelated. Interpreting them is an exercise in weaving our experiences together until they form a pattern that is comprehensible and, at times, consoling. If one is lucky, the digging and the musing over the findings are a way to achieve understanding and compassion, for oneself and for the people one loves.

I had a glimmer about where to dig next, or, as Naipaul would say, "a vibration." When I'd read aloud to my friend Arlene the passage where Vidia talks about Africans being "frightfully happy" to go back to their bananas and bongos—remarks insulting to Africans and patronizing to his wife—she'd said it seemed odd that Theroux had said nothing in return; there was something not quite right about it. I was reminded of other times when Vidia had said or done something that was obnoxious by any standard and Theroux had remained silent, though occasionally he does tell the reader he's uncomfortable. Two such incidents occur in a chapter of *Sir Vidia's Shadow* called "The 9:50 to Waterloo," which at the time I read it made me extremely uncomfortable and made me feel bad for Theroux; I wondered why he put up with such treatment. Something was going on there that needed to be looked into. I was pretty sure I would find out what it was.

8

"The 9:50 to Waterloo"

Strong wind, early darkness, and towering trees form the backdrop of this chapter of *Sir Vidia's Shadow*. Both Theroux and Naipaul have moved to the English countryside. Theroux and his family have rented a small cottage in an isolated part of Dorset, where Theroux works in a tiny second-floor room. Financially, he's just scraping by. The rented house Naipaul and his wife occupy stands on the grounds of a large estate in Wiltshire seventy miles distant, where the mentally unstable British landlord, whom they never see, has let black ivy engulf most of the trees, turning them into dark, half-dead presences.

When Theroux and his family arrive in Dorset, Naipaul jumps at the chance to invite him and Allison (the name Theroux gives to his wife, Ann) to lunch. Paul, nervous about the occasion, buys an expensive bottle of wine, explaining to the reader that Naipaul is a wine connoisseur. On the long drive to Naipaul's house, Theroux and Allison argue: Allison wants to move to London so she can get a job; he likes the country, is happy in his upstairs nook, and enjoys the company of the locals at the pub. As soon as they arrive, Naipaul senses something in the air, but Paul denies it. Vidia, obviously delighted to see Paul, praises him for his hard work (he's published several books since they last saw one another) and takes him off to show him his snuffbox collection. Allison is left to help with the lunch preparations—Pat is nervous about her cooking.

At the meal, Vidia makes himself obnoxious, downgrading American writers (Hemingway and Fitzgerald, Roth and Mailer), attacking "this bogus feminism" (Allison has dared to say something in defense of Zelda Fitzgerald), and belittling women in general: "Women long for witnesses, that is all," says Vidia. "Witnesses to their pleasure and their distress." After the meal, Vidia takes Paul on a long walk in the November dusk, naming all the bushes and trees, the grasses and wildflowers, leaving the women with the dishes. This makes Paul uncomfortable, but he does nothing about it. The final moment of the visit goes as follows— Paul and Allison are leaving:

> In the darkness outside, I heard Vidia whimper. Then he said, "I don't want you to go. I'll be depressed after you leave."
> "Vidia," Pat said in a soothing voice. He looked small and blurred in the rural darkness, and the wall of Wilsford Manor made the darkness greater, like a wall closing in behind us.

I love this moment for what it shows about the underside of the relationship: Vidia, ostensibly the strong one, is in fact forlorn, hungry for appreciation and support. His wife helplessly tries to appease his longing, and the darkness closing in foreshadows a more final separation between the friends.

A second lunch, which takes place in London, contains even more friction and builds to a climax more foreboding. It starts with Vidia, small and exotic, waiting on the Salisbury platform among English people who pointedly ignore him. He joins Paul, who has boarded ninety minutes earlier, and starts the conversation exactly where he did the last time: "Paul, Paul, you have something on your mind, I can tell."

> "No, I'm fine."
> "Your wife is not happy. I have a vibration."

"She wants to get a job."

"Good! Earn a few pence."

"What about you? How's things?"

"I have a broken wing."

Vidia can smell trouble at fifty paces, but although this time Paul tells him what's wrong, he doesn't pursue it. Naipaul switches the subject to his own exhaustion, his doubt that he'll ever write again. He asks Paul whom he's planning to see in London and when told exclaims: "Bogus, man. All bogus. They don't exist." He accuses Paul's acquaintances of "sucking energy" and "playing with art."

Paul pays for the taxis on their errands together, ending up at the Connaught, a restaurant where Naipaul had asked him to make reservations. As they enter, Paul picks up the telltale signs— uniformed porter and doorman, fresh flowers, a waiter "subservient in the bossy English way": it's going to cost a fortune.

In a supportive tone, Vidia assures Paul he'll do well in England; his reviews are valued, he'll be "recruited." He orders an expensive wine ("taste the chalk?"), nattering on about California roots (shallow) vs. French roots (deep). They order food, Paul taking the fish in order not to offend Vidia, a vegetarian. He asks Naipaul if Robert Lowell had been "recruited"—Vidia had been Lowell's guest for some time in New York. "I think Lowell is fraudulent, don't you?" says Vidia. Paul objects that the poems are good, but Vidia backs off, pretending not to be a judge of American poetry. He claims that, in any case, Lowell's visits to the psychiatric hospital are "a total con" and moves on to the subject of titles (Lowell's wife is an English Lady), making a little speech about their worthlessness. Interrupted in his harangue by the sound of a child crying in the hallway, Vidia expostulates against people who bring children to restaurants, calling it "a low peasant habit." Theroux shrugs, but recoils inwardly: "I felt like a coward for not telling him how fiercely I loved my children."

The meeting has become unpleasant enough, with Naipaul tossing off negative opinions right and left, ignoring his friend's feelings, but when the check arrives, things get worse. Naipaul seems too full of satisfaction in the wine and food to notice its existence, and, when Paul puts down four five-pound notes, says, "Oh, good," adding that it will cover the tip, since only people who are frightened of waiters tip them extravagantly. As they walk through the streets afterward, Naipaul becomes expansive and generous, as if to repay Paul for the lunch with flattery. Paul, for his part, hasn't enough money for his dinner and has to go home early. Nor can he buy his son the storybook he'd promised. He feels terrible but says nothing to Naipaul and very little to the reader. When they say good-bye he mentions, gratuitously, that he's going to hop a taxi to the *Times,* when in fact he can't afford a taxi and has to take a bus.

The scene at the Connaught echoes the lunch at Naipaul's house in Wiltshire and is a reprise of the one at the hotel in Kenya, where Theroux makes no response to Naipaul's treatment of Patsy or to his blatantly offensive "bananas and bongos" re-mark. This time Theroux's passivity is harder to understand. By now Theroux is an established writer, not a neophyte. He has a family, a position in the world, responsibilities. Theroux knows, having paid earlier for two taxis, that he can't afford to pay for the whole lunch, but he does it anyway and, during the conver-sation, allows Vidia to abuse him with nasty remarks about his London acquaintances, about Robert Lowell, whom he admires, and about people who take children with them when they go out for lunch. At that moment, Theroux says, he felt like a coward for not confessing how much he loved his children. But that isn't the half of it. His inability to stand up to his friend, his willingness to swallow insulting behavior, the cover-up of his financial situation and of his hurt at being manipulated cry out for explanation. None is forthcoming. Instead, the chapter ends with a stunning moment that anticipates the end of their relationship and at the same time sums it up:

> That night, without the new Ladybird book, I lay between my children and read them a story from one of the older books of fairy tales. . . . Outside, the wind from the sea at the end of the road tore at the bare boughs of our black oaks.
>
> With the children snuggled against me I read, "You don't understand the world, that's what's the matter with you. You ought to travel." And so they travelled, the shadow as master and the master as shadow, always side by side.

So much is going on in this chapter: on Vidia's part, so much neediness, and on Paul's, so much suppressed pain. The second time round it affected me even more deeply, though I still didn't know why. It was time to stop and make myself figure it out.

9

Shadow as Master and Master as Shadow

Reading pleasure has many sides to it, and one of them is definitely pain. The structure of the relationship between Naipaul and Theroux suggests various sinister analogies: perpetrator-victim, master-slave, parent-child (in its darker aspect). Readers who have occupied the second slot, psychologically—shadow, slave, child—more often than the first may resonate to Theroux's predicament. The shadow-slave-child position had been my default setting. When I think about it, the first thing that comes up is the excitement mixed with fear and shame I felt when I played house as a child with my friends Mary Ellen and Betty Ann Hayes. Someone would say, "Let's play house," and immediately shout, "Mother!"—which meant that she got to be the mother—the coveted role in our scenarios. If neither Betty Ann nor I could be mother, we liked it best when Mary Ellen was because she was so outrageous. She bossed us as if she'd been born to it and would threaten to do things so mean that we would crow with delight and horror. At such times Mary Ellen would occasionally allow a little smile to creep across her face, showing how pleased she was at her own ingenuity. I was always glad to see the smile because it reassured me that she wasn't as mean as she seemed to be but only pretending—though sometimes I wasn't sure.

There's a thrill in being dominated and pushed around—that's clear. It's courting danger and can be fun if you're only pretending. But Naipaul wasn't pretending, and Theroux's hurt was real; his intense embarrassment and humiliation, and the shame and anger that accompany them, give these scenes great force, and as I read about those lunches I was right there with him, because I know what it's like to be in his shoes. To put up with such treatment Theroux had to believe that Vidia had power over him, and that he, Paul, was vulnerable and dependent on Vidia for survival, as a child is upon his parent; otherwise his behavior makes no sense. The beliefs are unconscious, of course, but they're controlling him all the more for being so. Why else is every detail of these incidents burned into Theroux's memory—"bogus, man," "taste the chalk?" "a low peasant habit"? If you've ever been in Theroux's shoes it's easy to sympathize with his plight. You're the child, afraid to push back for fear of being punished or abandoned. Instead, tongue-tied and unable to sort out your feelings, you don't know if you've a right to be offended, and fear that if you react you might do something irrevocable. So you do what Paul did, hide what you feel, bide your time, hope that it all blows over, and continue to cling to the person who's mistreating you, because you believe you can't afford to lose them. For then who would be there to praise you when you succeed? Who would care? Besides, the hurt is familiar, so much a part of you you'd hardly recognize yourself without it, and, possibly, something you deserve. For Theroux, in *Sir Vidia's Shadow,* the parent figure, the idealized other, is Naipaul, though Naipaul must be standing in for someone in Theroux's past; otherwise, he'd have reacted differently. In my case, the first idealized person was my mother. But before I say anything about that, there's this to say about the way Theroux handles the material.

Given how wounded he was by the way Naipaul sometimes treated him, it's remarkable how well Theroux treated Naipaul in these re-creations of their lives. Theroux doesn't demonize him. At the same time that he shows us Naipaul hurting his feelings, he shows us how entertaining Naipaul's outrageousness is, how clever his wit, and how spontaneous his solicitude. He manages, miraculously, to keep everything more or less in balance. For while Theroux shows us that he accepts his abject position in these encounters and even enables it, he also shows us that he's aware of Naipaul's tremendous neediness. The moment when he and Allison get in the car at Wilsford Manor and hear Vidia speaking into the dark about how depressed he'll be now that Paul is leaving opens a sudden vista onto Naipaul's loneliness and fragility—as does the sight of him later standing alone at the train station, a small dark man being ignored by the other passengers. These scenes take place alongside the sickening glimpse we get of Naipaul's inflated self-regard when he attempts to repay Paul for lunch at the Connaught with flattering remarks about his work and future prospects. I started out being critical of Theroux for not speaking up when he should have. But when I realized that I had myself, in similar circumstances, done the same thing over and over, I began to sympathize with him, and have ended by admiring him for not mounting an all-out attack on Naipaul in revenge for what he'd suffered. The Naipaul he gives us is an unforgettable figure—brilliant, fond, witty, cruel, thoughtless, vulnerable, and never, ever, dull. The kind of person you're glad to see coming and—I imagine, if you were Theroux—glad to see going as well.

Theroux is not one for self-analysis or psychologizing, but at the end of the chapter on his lunches with Naipaul he offers a brilliant, schematic summing up of their relationship by quoting from the old book of fairy tales he read to his children. The image the excerpt offers, like the dancing dwarf in *Miguel Street,* resonates far beyond the confines of the moment.

With the children snuggled against me I read, "You don't understand the world, that's what's the matter with you. You ought to travel." And so they travelled, the shadow as master and the master as shadow, always side by side.

Though it's doubtful Theroux realized it was a metaphor for his friendship with Vidia back when he read the passage aloud to his boys, we know from the title of the memoir that it came to him eventually. But who is the master and who the shadow in this passage, and what does Theroux mean by it? There are so many meanings, and no way to decide. It can mean that although it looks as if the relation between the friends is one of domination and submission, and that Naipaul is the master and Theroux the shadow, that's not necessarily true, since master and shadow are interdependent and can change places—as in the moment when Paul and Allison are leaving Wilsford Manor. Master and shadow are separate, like Naipaul and Theroux, but can also be intrapsychic, two sides of the same person, where one side of the personality lords it over the other in imitation of a relationship the person has with someone outside himself, as when we scold ourselves for doing what the dominant other has scolded us for many times in the past. And it may not even be important which is which and who is who, which is Naipaul and which is Theroux. Master and shadow are figures in a fairy tale, not flesh and blood but symbolic, standing for ways of being that are universal and applicable to everybody at one time or another.

As I struggled to understand the relationship between Paul and Vidia, Theroux's image of master and shadow began to evoke ancient feelings in me, images I did not want to see, in which my mother is the master and I am the shadow, the reluctantly obedient servant, doing what I am told, fearing retribution and shame if I do not, obeying her, then my teachers, then anyone who held power over me, not objecting, not disobeying, not stepping out of line, but siding inwardly with those who do. The memories are not specific: they are structural. As I feel around in the dark for examples, I have hardly any individual recollections of my mother exercising power over me. Rather, it's a steady state, as if her power were so deeply entrenched it didn't need to show itself in any overt way. The only memory I have is of a moment—not specific but generalized—when, after I'd done something that displeased her, she gave me a threatening look and said reproachfully, "Jane, you *know* . . ." and that was enough. She didn't need to spell things out, much less raise a hand. The rules had been laid down long ago, in a time and in response to incidents beyond recall. My obedience was complete. All my mother had to do was remind me of what I already knew: resistance was hopeless. I picture myself in the kitchen, in the classroom, at Sunday school, in summer camp never doing anything that would bring down the wrath of whoever was in power over me, always good.

But these vague, powerful memories wouldn't have bothered me, or even have arisen, if the pattern they sprang from hadn't still been active in my life. Little by little, over the course of my engagement with Naipaul and Theroux, I began to see how my relationship to my husband paralleled Paul's relationship to Vidia. Though I didn't want to see the similarity, my visceral reaction to scenes like those lunches I've described forced to me acknowledge it. I tiptoed around the resemblance at first, but gradually the fact became unmistakable. The reason I had responded so strongly to the gift of *Sir Vidia's Shadow* was that the memoir mirrored a pattern of behavior etched into my own life. Like Theroux, I couldn't defend myself against aggression in a close relationship, whether with a spouse or a friend, because I was afraid of the consequences, just as I had been afraid to defend myself against my mother. And—it took me a while to make the connection—the reason for my fear was that I never wanted to go back to the place where I had spent the first six weeks of my life, which had taught me that anything was better than to be left alone.

I write about these discoveries calmly, as if the knowledge I came upon through my encounters with Naipaul and Theroux was somehow obvious or even self-evident, but it was not so. Again and again I revisited the pain of those lunches, again and again the closing words of the chapter, "the shadow as master and the master as shadow," reverberated in my mind. The persistence of these experiences prompted me to reread "The 9:50 to Waterloo" long after I had left *Sir Vidia's Shadow* behind, as I thought, and gone on to other books by the two men. Whether it was the rereading itself, or simply having lived so long with the question, "why does the relationship of these men haunt me so?" I don't know, but it was then that memories from my past began to arise—playing house with the Hayes kids, my mother's reproachful tone and glance, and, closer to home, fear of my husband's anger. And slowly the curtains began to open on the scene of my childhood relation to authority, a painful scene that was yet less painful than the alternative would have been—resistance, and the inevitable scolding and shaming and possible abandonment that I imagined would ensue. So it was by noticing the way my attention was drawn repeatedly to certain events and certain words in the text, and being willing to follow that lead, not knowing what lay ahead, trusting, and going in blind, that I came to understand, by piecing the fragments together, how the tracks of my fearful behavior in the present had been laid down long ago.

10

Reading Transformed

Reading had been many things to me—a source of energy, a spur to action, a medium of repose—but except for the occasional passage that shocked me into unwelcome knowledge of myself, never pursued and quickly forgotten, it had not been an avenue of self-discovery. As a child growing up, I had read to entertain myself and to escape from the world. Since I was shy and fearful, more comfortable on my bed at home with a book than on the playground or at school, I loved reading because it gave me contact with life without the need to take risks. At eight or nine, curled up in an uncomfortable chair in the dark living room of a house in the Catskill Mountains that belonged to friends of my parents, I struggled to follow the exploits of the young Natty Bumppo on a lake called the Glimmerglass, not understanding much of what I read but wrapped in the adventure, the danger, and the daring. Like Des Esseintes, the character in Huysmans's novel who plastered his room with travel posters but never went on vacation, I liked learning about people—Indians, for example—without having to meet them face to face, and going places without having to put up with the shocks of the material world. Whatever situation I was in, reading provided shelter from my immediate surroundings. If I didn't want to interact with people—my family, for instance—reading could be my haven. It was thousands of hours of unadulterated pleasure, free from social and emotional demands.

After it had become my stock in trade as an academic, reading still offered shelter. I chose a profession that compelled me to spend most of my time with books because that was what I enjoyed doing; I learned how to write about them and how to speak about them in public. Through books I kept the things I didn't understand or couldn't manage—my own emotional life and the rough-and-tumble of the world—at bay, though of course I didn't know that that was what was I doing. Since I'd taken up reading as a profession in part to protect myself from what was hurtful in both the inner and outer life, I never became the kind of reader who used reading and writing as an opportunity to plumb her own depths.

In the Spartan graduate student apartment—formerly home to the New Haven draft board—that I shared with my first husband, I read my way through the novels and tales of Henry James. They were not assigned in any of my courses, so it was a pastime requiring time and effort that I could ill afford, given how heavy the workload was in graduate school. But in truth, losing myself in Henry James was something I couldn't afford not to do. Though James was a respected author in what would become my field—American literature—I read him not for the sake of knowledge but, aside from the sheer pleasure of it, to shield myself from the rigors of a competitive graduate program and, though I was in love with my husband, from the unexpected loneliness of being married. James was a companion to whom I felt drawn for reasons I did not look into. His work became a refuge, his consciousness a domain where I loved to wander. James's view of the world became the standard by which I judged things. I wanted to be as discriminating in my thoughts, as sensitive in my perceptions, as impeccable in my moral behavior as he was. A year or two after getting my degree, I wrote two articles on James and edited an anthology of criticism on his famous novella *The Turn of the Screw*.

But never once did I ask myself why I couldn't tear myself away from stories about poor sensitive gentlemen who were invariably single, sexually repressed, and given to acts of renunciation. I went to James for the pleasure and the respite he afforded me, not for self-examination.

All of this is to say that if, as I tried to figure out what was going on between Naipaul and Theroux, their work became a mirror in which, increasingly, I found myself staring at my own reflection, it wasn't because this came naturally. It was a long time before I became interested, intellectually, in why a writer behaved as he or she did. And even longer before I started to ask why *I* reacted to a book in a particular way. That is, I had plenty of reactions to what I was reading, but I always attributed them to this or that feature of the text. Doing literary criticism meant backing up your opinions about a book by pointing to specific passages and describing what it was in them that bore you out. I'd never thought to ask what *in me* caused me to respond as I did. My relationship with my husband and my friendship with Maggie changed that.

Knowing Maggie had made me more aware of how people's childhoods determined the shape of their lives. Because she had had such a horrific childhood herself, Maggie took time to figure out why people acted the way they did, not in a casual, superficial way, but analytically. She looked beyond the surface they presented to how their experiences and conditioning had formed them. At the same time that I was absorbing from Maggie her X-ray vision approach to understanding people, I was forced to bring the same archaeological perspective to bear on myself; my husband and I had entered couples counseling in response to a crisis in our marriage. Despite years of psychotherapy, I didn't understand very much about where my own reactions to the world came from. This time, therapy allowed me to see that habitual ways of acting, both mine and my husband's, stemmed from how family circumstances over which we had no control had stamped and shaped us. It came as a surprise to discover how much of our makeup—from everyday habits to basic values and preferences—came directly from having grown up in a certain kind of household, and having absorbed the influences of the life around us. Contrary to what we'd assumed, who "we" were was far less the result of choices we made as freestanding individuals, than the result of biology, upbringing, social conditioning, and a particular concatenation of events. In other words, almost everything we did was motivated by forces we were unaware of, and couldn't be held responsible for, not, that is, until we became conscious of those forces and therefore able, at least sometimes, to exercise choice and exert some control over what we did.

This is a terribly abstract and somewhat clumsy way of talking about how people get to be who they are; the language is the technical, impersonal language of the social sciences—strange, given that the habits, tastes, feelings, and ways of talking that lie behind what I've been describing were the most personal things about us. But these abstract concepts got me to think about myself and my husband more reflectively than I had before, and influenced me unconsciously as I read Naipaul and Theroux. Hoping to find out why their story attracted me so much, I dared look at *why* I felt the way I did as a reader. When I finally realized that Theroux's pain and confusion when Naipaul treated him badly felt familiar to me because I had been in precisely that situation a thousand times, it changed my reading life, and as a result, the rest of my life as well. In trying to understand my own reactions at the same time I was trying to understand Theroux's, I finally, after all these years, had turned the critical lens on myself. My intense reaction to those lunches Theroux describes in *Sir Vidia's Shadow* forced me to recognize that, like him, when someone I was close to treated me badly, I couldn't push back or confront that person for fear I'd be cast out and left by the side of the road.

This realization, over time, brought about a shift in my marriage. Faced with my husband's anger, I no longer assumed automatically that I was at fault, no longer felt the knife go in so deep. Now there was distance between his words and my reaction, a coolness on my part, and a kind of neutral observation. "This man is angry now," I'd think to myself. "I wonder what's making him so angry?" And it would come to me that whatever it was, it wasn't what he was accusing me of, for he, too, was responding to patterns laid down long ago. At long last I'd stepped out of the victim role, the shadow, slave, child position. And for that I had *Sir Vidia's Shadow* to thank.

Once I saw myself in the text in this way, there was no going back. I recognized that my unconscious identification with an author—in this case, Theroux—and discovery that my life experience paralleled his was not a one-time thing, and that whether the author's experience was the same as mine or completely opposite, where reading was concerned, my past would always be in control. I saw that there was no way to read anybody's work that would not be just as telltale, that I would always, as a reader, be giving myself away by the nature of my reactions, and that it was impossible to read without—as we used to say in the heyday of literary theory—writing oneself into the text. I'd been going on the assumption that everything Theroux wrote, whether fiction or fact, in some way expressed his values and inclinations, that there was nothing on the page that was not an image of him. Fair enough. I'd always believed that. Well, now I saw that everything I thought and felt about his work reflected me.

I decided to experiment. I wanted to see how my newfound awareness as a reader would play out in relation to other books, not just books by Naipaul and Theroux. There were three books we had around the house that looked inviting—one a novel, one a work of literary criticism, one a collection of newspaper columns. I was going fishing—trying to catch a piece of myself in what I read. As long I caught something, anything, I'd be happy. Or so I thought.

☾

The first book, a highly praised novel by a contemporary European writer—Elena Ferrante's *The Days of Abandonment*—disturbed me so much that after a short while I had to put it down. I wasn't prepared for this. The story is about a woman whose husband has left her with no warning. As her living situation deteriorates, the main character falls apart and becomes increasingly self-destructive. She works herself into a frenzy; the prose—fevered, panicky, and wild—becomes painful to read. The protagonist's situation is bad, but her agonized consciousness makes it excruciating. I could hardly stand to live another minute inside this woman's head so I put the book aside, thinking that if I tried it again on another day, I might react differently. But when I picked it up again, if anything, it was worse. The second time I put the novel down, I put it down for good. Well, now, I could say to myself, this is just a story someone has made up. Why get so upset? Why? Because the whole point, in fiction, is to get you to live the experience as the protagonist lives it. Why else read? This book, because it ripped me up inside, made me realize once and for all that the emotional valence of a work of literature—the way reading it makes me feel—matters more to me than anything else. I'm not willing, simply because someone has recommended a book, or in order to keep up with the latest literary trend, to expose myself to pain. There was a time when I was willing to suffer for the sake of an intellectual or moral benefit I'd been assured of in advance. No longer. In order to simply live, I'd had to learn to protect my energy. For years, answering the demands of a work-oriented life, I had let intellect and will override body, heart, and spirit, but I could no longer afford to pay the price. My standard of judgment had shifted. Because all the doctors in the world had not been able to cure my illness, I had learned to be my own doctor. And this extended to my reading: if a book felt bad, it wasn't good for me, no matter what other people said. If I were going to read *The Days of Abandonment,* I might as well take poison.

Meanwhile, the sickening sensations I'd felt while reading the novel had taught me something about Naipaul and Theroux. I could read their work no matter what they were writing about, because each in his way was a rational presence maintaining at least the illusion of control over his own mind; neither would run the risk of exposing his readers to a process of mental disintegration, experienced from the inside, perhaps because neither could afford to risk undergoing the experience himself, even if it were only imagined. Sometimes the things Theroux and Naipaul write about are awful to contemplate, but the mode of delivery itself is safe. Though I might not share their attitudes, I could be sure that if I identified with the narrative point of view I would not be taken on a hair-raising ride that, whether or not it ended in a crash, wasn't worth the harrowing experience. My taste for readerly adventure was more limited than I had supposed. The contrast with Ferrante revealed Naipaul and Theroux as both, essentially, rationalist and conservative; though they might be severe as social critics—Naipaul is, anyway—they're not change-makers. Acute, intelligent, observant, devoted, and articulate, they are interpreters of the world, not movers and shakers in it, the kind of person you want to be your scout, not the one you send to secure the territory. Having started down this path, I saw that neither were they visionary, lyrical, romantic, or mystical—qualities I'd normally be attracted to. Having stumbled onto this realization, I backed away from it. I didn't want to go there. Sometimes, enough was enough.

To get away from the disintegrating narrator who'd been abandoned by her husband, I opened the book of criticism at random—it was *The Art of Intimacy* by Stacey D'Erasmo—and read a section on Elizabeth Bowen's *A House in Paris* that took my breath away. The writing was crystalline, the intellect stiletto-like, the sensibility exquisite. I was enthralled. Then I turned, at random, to a chapter which began with an attack on another critic—Vivian Gornick, as it turned out—an attack whose ferocity was so far out of proportion to what had ignited it, I could barely believe it had come from the author of such limpid prose and subtle insights. D'Erasmo took the very existence of Gornick's position to be an outrage directed at her. The attack upset me. I, too, was overreacting. It was time to quiet down. After an interval I came back to the book and read it from start to finish. Except for the defensive assault I've mentioned, the book was just as good as I'd thought: eye-opening, brilliant, superbly written. When did literary criticism become so readable?

D'Erasmo writes on Lawrence's *The Rainbow,* Conrad's *The Secret Sharer,* Nella Larsen's *Passing,* and William Maxwell's *So Long, See You Tomorrow,* among other books, always in a manner that is probing, nuanced, and full of allure. Her subject, intimacy—unusual and little noticed—brings us in so close to moments in our experience as readers it's as if no one had ever gone there before, and it does so with a degree of refinement seldom matched in criticism. D'Erasmo is a genius at putting words to things we may have sensed in a book but could never quite apprehend. It wasn't just her fine perceptions and supple prose that impressed me, it was also her tone—delicate and sensitive, feminine and slightly seductive, yet knowing and sure of itself, imperious, almost. I wanted to *be* her as I read. There was so much beauty here—beauty of conception and beauty of execution—a great tide of admiration and appreciation welled up inside me and flowed out in her direction. And then it halted. All at once another feeling took its place. I had spent a good part of my life writing literary criticism, and it struck me that I'd never written anything as good as *The Art of Intimacy* and never would. It wasn't fair. She was young and I was old and feeling washed up. Envy had taken possession.

Oh, envy. This was not the first nor would it be the last time a book had made me envious. My envy had nothing to do with the books themselves, of that I was sure. Envy was an old habit laid down long ago. At seven or eight, I envied my cousin Jane Alice as we danced around the living room to the music of *The Nutcracker Suite*—coming, if I'm not mistaken, from a machine called a phonograph, which had just replaced the Victrola—envious because I'd overheard my mother remark on how graceful my cousin was, and I wanted to be the one who was graceful. I envied the girls in my class at P.S. 98 whose blouses and skirts were fresher and more crisply ironed than mine. I envied children who had brothers and sisters: they had a group, a tribe, a cohort to belong to, while I had only myself. I envied the Hayes kids, who lived upstairs in my apartment building, for being Catholic—they had family prayers and went to a dark and shining, colorful, incense-filled place on Sundays, thronged with other people; it was like belonging to a universal family—whereas my mother, my father, and I, with no religion, were out there on our own. I saw everywhere people who had things that, in my eyes, made them loved, admired, and protected. To my own privileges I was blind.

Criticizing oneself for being envious does not do anything to remove the habit. Envy stings. Envious persons need tenderness and mercy; they need reassurance and love. They feel deprived and ill-treated, which makes them feel wounded, bitter, and greedy; they need to get in touch with their softer feelings; they need emollients to remove the sting.

A story I read in the *New York Times* one day did this for me. Don DeLillo, a winner of the National Book Award, had just been given a Medal for Distinguished Contribution to American Letters. "He was typically understated in his acceptance speech," the story said. "Rather than talking about his work or his evolution as a writer, he spoke reverently about a room where he keeps his collection of old paperbacks. 'When I visit the room, I'm not a writer,' he said. 'That's the guy who lives down the hall. Here I'm not the writer at all, I'm the grateful reader.'"

The cure for envy is to be able to be grateful, to know how to receive. No matter how deprived one may be, there is always something there to be received if only one can see it. Though an award-winning writer, as a reader DeLillo was not self-important or self-regarding; he was humble and accepting of the gifts of others. When I saw this, something in me softened. If a man like DeLillo could be accepting and humble, it made me want to be that way, and I realized that I, too, was a grateful reader, who had, metaphorically at least, inhabited that room of DeLillo's, though I might not always be able to have a grateful heart.

The longer I thought about it, the more I began to suspect that although envy is in the eye of the beholder, there are some books that are more likely to arouse it than others. Stacey D'Erasmo's writing, in addition to being beautiful, is a virtuoso performance. As her reader, I'm always noticing how intelligent she is, how gifted, how skillful. Writing that calls attention to the writer's skill subtly sets itself off from its readers by asking for their admiration. An obligation to admire the performance interposes itself between us and the subject. At least sometimes it does. When I read Proust, I am ravished by his skill, but I never feel envious. Perhaps the personality of the writer is involved as well. Sometimes, the interposition of the writer's personality can have a welcoming, enlivening effect, as, for example, when Melville's exuberance carries him away in prolonged and elaborate encomiums of the whale. But sometimes, as in the case of D'Erasmo's prose, it can make one feel separate and apart. It's like looking at the face of a beautiful woman: sometimes her beauty can make you feel close to her, invited in, and sometimes it can make you feel excluded, reminding you that you are not as beautiful as she. And of course which qualities will arouse such feelings and which will not depends upon the reader. It happened that the third book on my experimental list, *Alligators in B-Flat,* a collection of essays about Florida by a seasoned journalist named Jeff Klinkenberg, helped make these distinctions clearer.

Klinkenberg had honed his skills writing for newspapers. His sentences are taut and packed, his timing perfect, his ability to create momentum unparalleled; he delivers a great punch line, he cuts to the chase. I loved reading his stuff. But. He was a journalist: I had never been a journalist nor had I ever aspired to be one. His subject matter was miles from anything I'd ever written about. He was a man with an outdoorsy image and a folksy idiom—not my territory. No wonder I felt no competition with him. Does the swan envy the tiger? Stacey D'Erasmo, on the other hand, wrote on books I had used in my courses, in a language I was familiar with; she taught at Columbia University, where I had once taught. It's classic. One always envies the person who does what's closest to what one does oneself. But there was more to it than that.

In his craft, Jeff Klinkenberg is the equal of Ferrante and D'Erasmo in theirs. Though he lacks the novelist's passion and the intellectual brilliance of the literary critic (also a novelist), his writing has a quality that isn't completely absent in the other writers but predominates in his—a human warmth and generosity toward its subjects. Klinkenberg refrains from judgment. He creates air and space around the people and places he writes about so that they seem to be speaking for themselves. His attitude is appreciative rather than analytic or interpretive, the style so self-effacing you hardly know he's there, and though sometimes he'll joke around a bit, the joke is always on him. The odd characters and funky settings he describes seem to come alive on their own. Here, for example, is a short paragraph describing the atmosphere of a place he likes to visit, Joanie's Blue Crab Café, the only restaurant in the 725,000-acre Big Cypress National Preserve:

> Her loyal regulars, as long as I have been going there, have included cane-pole fishermen stinking of bream, Miccosukees who like her fry bread, and legions of foreign tourists who have worked up an appetite by counting alligators along the road. "I parlez-vous with people pretty easy," Joanie told me.

I would love to be able to write a paragraph like that.

Along with Joanie, the author introduces us to a series of quixotic characters: Thunderman, a blind man who loves thunder, records it, predicts the weather by it, and listens to it alive or on tape, whenever he can, transfixed. He writes about Flip-Flop Man, who runs and walks from place to place all day and sometimes all night, always wearing flip-flops, traveling an average of 6,500 miles a year. Flip-Flop Man has trouble standing still. In another column Klinkenberg tells us about black men in Florida who, after the devastating hurricane of 1928, were expected to clean up the wreckage for no pay. Though he stays in the shadows, being in this man's presence feels good—not because he encourages or reassures his readers, caters to us or flatters us, as writers sometimes do, but because he holds up pieces of the world that are a cause for wonder. Without glossing over the hard parts—poverty, sickness, violence, mental instability—he captures the qualities that make his subjects one-of-a-kind, celebrates their passions and understands their obsessions—their truth shines out, it would seem, without any mediation at all. And what's left is an essence that is something like pure joy.

There's a moral quality, an effect of character that is always coming through writing that imprints itself on the mind and soul. Reading columns by Jeff Klinkenberg, I can feel my attitude toward the world being cleansed and purified. Everything is clearer and brighter than before. I'd been having this experience for a long time in response to spiritual books like Shunryu Suzuki's *Zen Mind, Beginner's Mind* or Rachel Remen's *My Grandfather's Blessings*. Klinkenberg's work appears in daily newspapers; his motto could well be William Carlos Williams's famous dictum: "no ideas but in things." This writer reveals the depth of his subject through a brilliant choice of surface details, but he has also internalized the spirit of his subjects and breathed that into his prose. He's channeling the people he writes about, not just putting words on paper. And there was another reason I was taken by Jeff Klinkenberg that had nothing to do with him.

I had never liked Florida. Klinkenberg's columns warmed me to it for the first time. The reason appeared in a blurb on the back of his book: "his stories belie the ghastly six-lane, strip-mall, gated-community, golf-coursed, air-conditioned, theme-parked nature-wrecking Florida that most of its citizens know." That is why I loved Klinkenberg. He gave me something unhomogenized I could latch on to. The blurb writers all say that Klinkenberg loves the "old" Florida, the Florida of the Gladesmen, of swamps and alligators, cottonmouths and panthers. And that's true. But his real gift lies in finding the genius of plain people like Wendy Johnson, the bossiest woman who ever lived, and Jim Long, the golf fanatic who died next to the tenth hole as he was about to putt for birdie. These sketches are not swathed in Spanish moss or bathed in moonlight. "Riding a golf cart was [Jim's] primary form of exercise. He ate too much Breyers vanilla ice cream and watched too much TV. On the night before he died, [his wife] fixed him his favorite meal: grilled chicken and fresh corn cut from the cob. He feared no pat of butter."

"He feared no pat of butter." You can't beat that. Klinkenberg gave me something to put next to the luxury cars, face-lifts, ocean-front condos, and swanky restaurants. There was Thunderman, there was Wendy Johnson, there was Joanie's Blue Crab Café.

Once, when we were vacationing on Florida's west coast, my husband and I went to Joanie's: Joanie wasn't there anymore; it was her granddaughter we spoke to, but the atmosphere was pretty much what Klinkenberg had described, minus the Miccosukee Indians; there was a lone guitarist playing at lunchtime, and the steamed shrimp were excellent. After I finished, I wandered around looking at the old Florida souvenirs and fell into conversation with a woman in her sixties, traveling by herself since her husband died; she was staying in that part of the Everglades for a few months, exploring. If I'd been Jeff I could have written a column.

Neither Naipaul nor Theroux offers the clarity of vision that energizes the work of the newspaperman; they don't celebrate life as he does. But they give of themselves in their writing as much as or more than most writers, not through explicit self-disclosure, but wholeheartedly. For both of them writing is a way of life and a means of self-construction. Dedicated to the craft for its own sake—doing it because they are called to do it—relying on the craft as a means of making a living, they use writing to testify to their experience and to enter into relations with the world. For them, writing is a way to bring themselves into existence and to maintain themselves in it. They live in and through it. They risk exposure, they pour out their energy and effort, they exercise fortitude and discipline: over and over again, they try to get it right. Like Thunderman, like Flip-Flop Man, like Wendy Johnson, and golf man Jim Long, they're faithful to their obsession, and ennobled by it. I wasn't through with them yet.

11

My Other Life

When we met for lunch on Mondays at the French bakery, Maggie was always there first. I would arrive either on time or a little late, it being a principle with me to avoid having to wait alone. Though later on she told me she was always early because she had a lifelong fear of being late, to me her promptness meant that our lunches were important to her—they certainly were to me. Writing this book was providing me with a reason for being, and Maggie was my lifeline. Perhaps it was her twenty-three years as an attorney, perhaps it was because she was that rare person, a real grown-up, but whatever the reason, she spoke about my work with such authority and in such a wise and reassuring tone, that I put all the faith I had in her pronouncements. She spoke about Theroux. As the breeze blew through the arches and the sparrows hopped about, pecking at pastry crumbs—the coffee and pastries were excellent at the Côté France—she spoke enthusiastically about the three great early chapters of the book she had recently given me, though there was mention of a recurrent problem, something to do with women.

My Other Life is a semi-fictional memoir by Theroux published two years before *Sir Vidia's Shadow,* and when I read those three great chapters, I didn't see any problem. At least not in the beginning. I enjoyed the book so much it became *my* other life. I was off on a series of adventures in the company of a sympathetic, intelligent man who revealed his emotional life in a way that made me feel much closer to him than I had previously. The writing was superb, and the book gave me just what I wanted—adventure and intimacy all in one.

Theroux calls the book a novel, titles it "My *Other* Life," but since it's written in the first person, and he uses his own name, and most of the material comes from his own life, it's hard to approach the book as fiction. For whatever reason, Theroux needs to write about himself, but he doesn't want to be held accountable for what he reveals. For a reader, it's confusing. There's no way to tell the difference between what's real and what's invented. So I read the book the way that felt most natural, which is to say, as if it really happened; some of the facts were undoubtedly changed, but because of its emotional substance it feels as if it's true. Reading it was an intense and memorable experience. *My Other Life* is so much better than *The Old Patagonian Express* and *The Great Railway Bazaar:* there's no more watching the world from train windows, punctuated by superficial interactions with strangers. Now, real things are happening to Theroux, and he's letting us in on how it feels.

"The Lepers of Moyo"

In the book's first real chapter, Paul, a young English instructor teaching in Africa, has chosen to spend his vacation teaching at a leper colony farther back in the bush. Theroux names the leper colony "Moyo," and his description of it is unforgettable: "The reality here was that no one was sentimental. They came here ill; they declined; they died. No one advanced or prospered. It was a small world in which no one had the illusion of making choices. And no one minded that. I did not know why this was so, though I suspected that it was because the people here were always in the presence of death."

For the first time in his life, Theroux has encountered a world that has nothing to do with the things that until then he must have considered important: becoming educated, making a good living, being recognized by the world for his accomplishments. None of these things is possible in Moyo. The people there have no place to go and no way to change their lives. Nobody is looking at them, and they are not looking for approval from anyone else. There is birth, copulation, and death, and in the meantime, subsistence living with no alternative in sight.

After a short while, Paul, who's an aspiring poet, decides to dig a hole and bury his poems along with the Kafka *Diaries* he's been reading. His poems now seem artificial and self-conscious, and Kafka seems like a narcissistic hypochondriac. When Kafka writes in his diary, "Sometimes I feel like a leper," Theroux writes:

> Kafka was not a leper. He was a middle-class insurance clerk with a batlike face, pathologically timid and paranoid and guilt-ridden, . . . [someone who] wrote long fussy letters to lonely women desperate for the chance to love him.

Having seen real lepers, Paul regards Kafka as a deluded weakling. He remarks that staying in Moyo could turn a person off literature altogether because the lepers, who have to remain at Moyo eking out a bare existence, can have nothing that the wider world of culture offers. Though Theroux may be idealizing their rejection of Western civilization, he's taking his discovery seriously and acting from his new beliefs. I respected him for this. Before long he gives up teaching English altogether and starts building a kitchen that a priest who had formerly been at Moyo had begun.

In the course of burying his poems, Theroux disturbs a couple in the act of lovemaking. Though the woman runs off, Theroux is able to have a conversation with the man, whom he ends up asking to help make bricks for the new kitchen. The man asks how much he'll be paid. When Theroux says, "Nothing," and the man refuses to help, Theroux comments:

> This was a leper: guiltless, maimed, seeping into his bandages . . . now staring me down. . . . He was patient and contemptuous because he was powerless and he knew it. Perhaps he knew that nothing would change for him, nor would he change anything. He had no illusions, and so he was fully alive every waking moment, looking for food or water, looking for shade, looking for a woman.

Theroux doesn't take the refusal personally; he's able to imagine how this man's lack of what Westerners call a future forces him to live in the moment and gives his life an intensity and fullness that Theroux's own life lacks. Nothing short of brute force can compel the man to do anything he doesn't want to, for, from someone like Paul, he has nothing to gain or lose. No moral suasion, no appeal to community values, no invocation of any value known to the narrator can make him budge an inch. He embodies the absolute; there is nothing beyond him.

The priests who have devoted their lives to serving the colony share the lepers' absence of illusions. They've given up on Western culture as well, and it's not only reading and writing they no longer believe in. When Paul tells Father DeVoss of his plan to make bricks for the kitchen, the Father Superior gives his approval but seems not to care. He smiles and says, "The kitchen and the bricks were Father LeGrande's idea. . . . He is now in Basutoland." That the person who thought up the idea of a new kitchen is now somewhere else implies that nothing anyone can do can make a difference. Father LeGrande could make no difference, and neither can Paul. Any actions of his will make a difference only to himself.

Before long Paul realizes that Father DeVoss, a man revered

by everyone, no longer puts much store in his own religion. He performs the rituals of the Mass listlessly, forgets the words of prayers, leans on the altar with his elbows:

> He seemed bored when he was saying mass, but it was the intense reflection of a scientist sweeping the laboratory floor. His face was blank, but a pitiless light burned behind his eyes. He believed in himself; therefore he did not need to believe in God.

Theroux doesn't mean that the priest has come, like Conrad's Kurtz, to think that he *is* God, or even that he is no longer a spiritual leader—on the contrary—but that the priest no longer needs the outward expressions of his faith because he has internalized its teachings to a point where he simply enacts them without having to think about it. Theroux, a former altar boy raised by a mother fanatically devoted to the church, is inspired and captivated by Father DeVoss's lack of outward piety, and by the force of his presence: "When Father DeVoss was happy . . . it showed on everyone's face. It was yet another instance of his power, that his spirit was felt throughout the leprosarium."

But while he admires the spiritual presence of a Father DeVoss, Paul is far from being able to live as the priest does. Among the nuns who treat the lepers with medicine and bandages is one who isn't a nun but a volunteer who wears a nun's habit. This woman, whom Theroux calls Birdie, is older than he, somewhere in her early thirties. One day she suggests that they picnic together on the shores of a lake—Paul has the use of a motor scooter. When they arrive, Theroux decides he doesn't want to stay—it's getting late—so they decide to picnic in Birdie's room instead. He has to sneak up the stairs so the nuns won't know, and finds himself trapped. Birdie has changed into her nun's habit—with nothing on underneath—and starts pretending that he's going to rape her, whispering things like "Don't touch me, Father" (Paul is wearing a soutane that Father DeVoss lent him to impress the locals at the toll gates). They become entangled in each other's long white robes and, after some clumsy maneuvering, he pushes her away, realizing that he neither desires nor particularly likes Birdie. They end up lying on her bed, while outside in the corridor, the nuns are walking by, talking to each other. Paul wants more than anything to get out of there but has to wait for hours until the nuns go to sleep. The situation is unbearably awkward and painful—and ridiculous.

The next thing we know, Paul yields to the advances of a beautiful fifteen-year-old village girl named Amina, formerly a student in his English class. In an overheated and embarrassing scene—embarrassing for the reader, that is—the two copulate in front of her blind grandmother while, at a distance, the lepers, in their nightly ritual, beat drums and dance—the scene has an orgiastic feel to it—chanting phrases from the Mass, a different kind of transgression from the one being enacted in the grandmother's hut and, if Theroux invented it, which I suspect he did, equally tasteless. Afterward, Paul can't stay in Moyo. Somehow, everyone knows what's happened. He can't marry the girl, or become a nurse, or be a priest like Father DeVoss, and there's no more English class; he has to leave the village.

Given the dramatic nature of the incident with Amina, Theroux has surprisingly little to say about it or about his unfortunate entanglement with the nurse: this troubled me. If these things really happened, he doesn't display much curiosity about his participation in them, and if, as a professional writer in his fifties, he invented them, they're even harder to explain. I decided not to get sidetracked by what could be an aberration. The young Paul has made some mistakes, but in the leper colony he's also had a glimpse of something more real than anything he has yet encountered in his life, and he lets it alter him. As the train pulls out of Moyo, Paul reflects:

> The lepers and priests and nuns, all of them, were happier than anyone I had ever met. They had found what they were looking for. What luck. It bothered me that I had not been able to fit in; that through my own fault I had been cast out; and that having left I would have to keep going—searching for the rest of my life for a similar place, and my mind always returning to Moyo.

I breathe a sigh of relief. Moyo let me see that Theroux has a depth of perception not apparent in his travel books, and a spiritual insight that had remained submerged in *Sir Vidia's Shadow*. He recognized how lucky people are who have found their life's vocation and can devote themselves to it wholeheartedly. I saw him as a seeker, hungry for a glimpse of things that went beyond his understanding, able to question the values of his upbringing. I envied him the experience and doubted that, if I'd had the same exposure at his age, I'd have understood as much. The man who had written about Moyo was not only going places by getting on planes and trains, he was in the process of deepening his inner life, allowing his experience to penetrate and change him. Although the incidents involving women gave me pause, I wanted to go with him on his adventures. The vision he gave me of the life lived by the lepers of Moyo and by those who cared for them was indelible.

"Poetry Lessons"

"I did not understand anything I read, nor did I begin to write any better, until I married and had children." So begins the chapter of *My Other Life* called "Poetry Lessons," the second of the three great chapters Maggie had put me on to. Marriage and fatherhood have deepened Theroux. He's found out that experience is not simply the best but the only teacher. His memories of the years he spent with his young family in Singapore are fresh and penetrating. He went there because he wanted to be near the Vietnam War, which he opposed, had a hankering to see Southeast Asia, and felt the attraction of an old colonial city. On the practical side, it was also a place where he could get a job—he was now in debt.

Theroux teaches English at the University of Singapore, which doesn't pay much, his wife teaches at Nanyang, the Chinese University, and still they still have trouble making ends meet. Their small house is full of traffic fumes and the sounds of buses. They can't afford a car and don't even have enough money to go to the movies. But the exoticism of the locale makes up for a lot. I love the names of streets and places—Jurong Road, Bukit Timah Road, Luck Ong's camera shop, Chop Heng Fatt Keng (provisioners), and, across from his home, Serene House—the building where U.S. servicemen came on their week's furlough to be serviced by prostitutes at government expense. He entertains us with conversations overheard at the Staff Club of the university, full of disgruntled lecturers who brag about how drunk they'd gotten the night before and who practice being rude to newcomers—the rudest are the most admired. "He's a rat bag" is their highest compliment, one that always reminds Theroux of how much he hates the place and wants to leave. But he can't afford to. The economic pressures of the writer's life are getting to him.

One day Theroux takes his family to a deserted house on the Jurong Road to drop off a key for a friend, recently divorced. The house, two-storied with verandahs on all sides, standing in a tropical grove, is much nicer than his own; Allison (the same name he gives his wife, Ann, in *Sir Vidia's Shadow*, which is a memoir, not a novel) says that she wishes it were theirs. But when they look inside, the mood changes. Malacca chests, an empty fruit bowl, an empty vase, children's toys lovingly propped, bright pillows placed just so—these are the abandoned possessions of what had once been a family. They make Theroux intensely aware of his own happiness. He grabs his wife and kisses her with all the love in his heart. "We have everything," he thinks to himself. He can't wait to get out of there. The scene ends:

> Ringrose's house represented failed hopes, an ended life, the stage set without a play, all the actors gone, never to return. This glimpse gave me a horror of divorce: the loss, the pain, the emptiness. A family split up and scattered. You could not lose more than this.

The moment cuts him to the quick. But he writes with such feeling because, as we learn later in the book, he is now going through a divorce himself and knows at first hand the pain he's referring to. The moment conveys the deep love he has for his wife and children and the depth of his loss.

But at the time he's writing about, the divorce is far in the future. Soon Paul will better his situation. At one of the embassy parties he's invited to, he meets an American businessman in the library and they begin speaking of books. When the businessman, Harry Lazard, discovers that Paul is a poet and teaches literature, Lazard, who's interested in poetry and has published a few poems of his own, offers Paul a deal: in exchange for giving poetry lessons to Lazard, Paul can live with his family rent-free on Lazard's estate. Not only will it mean gracious quarters for his wife and children, it also means Paul can do what he's wanted for so long: quit his job and write full-time. He accepts. The estate has a pool where Paul first meets Lazard's predatory wife, a pool around which his children can romp, "Allison's face light with love as she watched them." There's a screened verandah where the family eats their meals, a lawn where they play croquet. You feel the warmth of his happiness as he recalls these moments.

But the whole setup is poisoned from the start. Paul learns that Lazard makes his money in the war, and that he had bribed the editor of the magazine that published his poems. Though Lazard enjoys Paul's talk about poetry, when it comes to his own writing he wants validation rather than instruction or critique, an attitude Paul finds hard to tolerate. But latent hostility to his host has been there all along. It underlies almost all his conversations with Lazard, whom he flatters and has contempt for. Because in their exchanges Lazard does not immediately see Paul's point of view, and because his taste in poetry is unsophisticated ("his style, if such a word could apply to flat declarative statements, was artless, almost crude"), Theroux considers himself the superior person and assumes the reader will, too. On first reading the chapter, I agreed, looking down on Lazard because his poems were bad, and his taste undeveloped. But the second time round I drew back.

Theroux's scorn for his employer is venomous. Like many intellectuals he sneers at people with money simply because they have it and because they know less than he does about cultural matters. For Allison's and the boys' sake, Theroux keeps his views about Harry to himself, but he can't help making a fool out of him in nasty asides to the reader.

> [Lazard is speaking] "Have you been doing some writing?"
>
> "Working on my novel."
>
> "That's good."
>
> "It's going well, thanks to . . ." I did not know how to finish the sentence. Thanks to your being away. Thanks to this luxurious estate. Thanks to your wife, who hardly speaks to us. Thanks to my nervous anxiety in wanting to finish the book and be solvent.

"Maybe you could put in a little note or something at the beginning—how we helped you out," Harry said.

There was not even the slightest undertone of irony in his voice, and his smug, beaky face had never looked more proprietorial. He was serious! And though I objected, and once again wanted to quit, I swallowed hard. I had a family to support. I was his prisoner. I looked at him, hardly believing his hubris, and thought: You wish.

"Or maybe dedicate it to you," I said.

I knew he would not accuse me of mocking him. Someone incapable of expressing irony was equally incapable of hearing it.

As he writes the scene, years later, Theroux is getting his licks in, taking it out of Harry's hide because he, Paul, had felt humiliated by having to be polite to someone he had little respect for. He's still angry, as he writes, and needs to vent his spite.

The tension between them—the successful electronics manufacturer living on profits from the Vietnam War who wants to broaden his horizons, and the young man who needs a break from the grind of poverty in order to pursue his dream of becoming a novelist—the misunderstanding, the desire, and, at least on Theroux's part, the deceit, make for wonderful scenes. It's what Theroux does so brilliantly in *Sir Vidia's Shadow* in re-creating his encounters with Naipaul. But while in *Sir Vidia's Shadow* he lets us see his pain at being treated badly, his fear of rejection and inability to confront his friend, here he takes it for granted that we'll recognize his superiority to Lazard and share his outrage at being, as he thinks, toyed with by his patron. Theroux thinks Harry Lazard is ignorant because he lacks a sense of literary style, and venal because he profits from the war, but can't see how inflated his own self-image is, and how self-serving his attitude. From having been enthralled by the story of a young writer making his way in an exotic locale, I began to be put off. It wasn't fun anymore identifying with Theroux. As the chapter ends, things get worse.

One day when Paul enters the main house in search of the owner, Lazard's wife, Fayette, calls him into the bedroom and makes a flagrant pass at him, practically commanding him to have sex with her, all the while ridiculing her husband's attempt at self-improvement. When Paul refuses her point-blank, she insults him ("What do you think we pay you for?") and tells him to get out. When Theroux realizes that the price of staying in the cottage will probably be an affair with Lazard's wife, he decides to leave. But not before stealing a valuable artifact that Fayette had misplaced.

Theroux steals the artifact—a child's death mask made of the costliest jade—out of revenge, and out of indignation at having been propositioned by an older woman—not his sexual equal—and perhaps out of economic need. Theroux is not like Strether in *The Ambassadors,* whose claim to integrity is "not out of all this to have gotten anything for myself." He's exactly the opposite. Theroux considers himself justified in robbing his employers and refers to the jade piece as "the spoils of war." Theroux may have been vindictive and greedy because he had a family to support and needed the money, which Strether did not. Still, his behavior is shocking, if it did occur; and if it didn't, why did Theroux have his protagonist strike back in this underhanded way? I was having trouble getting a handle on my relationship to Theroux. When he expresses love for his wife and children, I feel its depth and intensity; when he takes potshots at Lazard, I'm sympathetic at first, then back away, repelled by his arrogance; when he expresses distaste at Fayette's advances, I can understand why initially, and then am put off by the strength of his revulsion.

But things became even more complicated when I started remembering a piece of my own history. Suddenly I knew why Theroux acted as he did toward his landlord. In literary and cultural fields, it's not unusual to flatter yourself that you're better than people who happen to lack your knowledge and achievements. The belief need not register as such, at least it didn't for me—I considered myself too nice a person — but the need to feel, and to be seen as, superior motivated me all the same. As a young professor married to another young professor, I would place myself at faculty dinner parties firmly with the faculty members, almost always men, so as not to be confused with their wives. Mere appendages of their husbands (or so I thought), they wore unfashionable clothes and, with few exceptions, didn't take part in discussions of intellectual or professional matters. If they did, I considered them upstarts and a threat. Not that I was any brilliant conversationalist; I simply didn't want the competition. I was completely identified with my academic position as an assistant professor of English, and although I was a daughter and a wife and a friend, didn't think I had anything to offer the world but my degrees, my job, and my publications, meagre though they were.

Being publicly associated with Lazard was as unthinkable for Theroux as it was for me to be mistaken for a faculty wife. As he makes mean-spirited wisecracks to the reader at Lazard's expense, it's my old self I see, one of the underappreciated, underrewarded junior professors of the world, seething with a sense of injured merit. When you're just starting out in life, think you've found your niche, and are putting everything you have into gaining a foothold, you act with single-minded ferocity, not daring to relax even for second, lest you lose your balance and fall back into nothingness.

But not every young writer is snide and dismissive of those who are less literate; not every assistant professor looks down on people who don't have an academic post. What was missing in Theroux and in me that made us depend so heavily on a thin sliver of professional identity? I don't know. I do know that I once shared Theroux's insecurity and desire to appear meritorious, so I had to cut him some slack. Little as I liked seeing myself reflected in this unattractive way, I couldn't take it out on him. It wasn't fair.

"Lady Max"

After he left Singapore, Theroux settled in London, where, as he tells us in the chapter called "Lady Max," he still felt like an outsider, despite having lived there for seven years. As the chapter opens, he thinks he's getting his foot in the door when he discovers Gaston's, a little-known book shop he'd been introduced to by Ian Musprat. Musprat, a poet whom he identifies as the author of *The Dogflud Chronicles,* is a British literary type, seedy, down on his luck, badly dressed, depressed, and irritable. A foil for Theroux—who by contrast seems to represent some norm of good nature, common sense, and decent table manners—Musprat functions as a one-man Greek chorus, commenting disgustedly on the vanity and corruption he sees around him. I found him so unappealing I wished he would go away, and he does, but later on, after the main action of the chapter has occurred, he returns, with some crucial information.

What transpires between Musprat's first and last appearances is the story of how Theroux, living happily with his family in a Victorian house in Clapham, allows himself to be taken up by the wife of an absent peer. Lady Max is beautiful and well-connected. She shows him the London he doesn't know—hidden back streets, obscure churches and museums, the houses where famous people have lived. When he becomes elusive in response to her repeated invitations, she gets him offers of work from magazine editors and favorable publicity for his books, a state of affairs he very much enjoys. Gradually she begins to make sexual advances, which Theroux gently rebuffs, but not before he has begun to feel manipulated and used, even in some way soiled, by her.

The chapter pivots on the tension between Theroux's home life and Lady Max: on the one hand, the sense of fulfillment he feels in his work and family, and on the other, his experiences with the adventuress, who is beautiful, seductive, and cruel. Lady Max's world is sinister and captivating—she makes a great villainess—but Theroux's description of his home life is even more compelling. When he describes himself sitting safe in his high room, looking out over the black chimneys and slate roofs of London, writing about life in the jungles of Honduras, warm despite the bleak cold weather, comfortable amid grimy brick and stone, his satisfaction and contentment are palpable. At four o'clock he shops for the evening meal, stopping at a pub for a beer on the way home. His sons arrive from school, have their cookies and milk, and do their homework at the kitchen table as he moves from counter to stove, chopping onions and peppers for spaghetti sauce, sautéing the garlic, watching the tomatoes bubble. His wife returns after her day of work, and they sit down together to the meal. I feel Theroux relishing every moment as he re-creates these scenes, the act of description an homage to the life he lived then, and a consecration of it. The scenes have the aura of precious objects carefully preserved and fondly displayed. Warmth and contentment fill me when I read them, and I share his sense of fulfillment, perhaps all the more because I was never able to have children of my own. Theroux lets me see and feel what it could have been like.

His London social life is a different story. He attends receptions and openings where Lady Max is present, visits museums and little-known London attractions with her, and goes to a ghastly dinner party she presides over. I'm enthralled by the view of literary London and want to know more, but disturbed as well, dismayed as much by Theroux's behavior as by the domineering, greedy way that Lady Max pursues him, galled and spurred as she is by his failure to reciprocate her interest. He half-succumbs to the glamour she represents—class, beauty, money, connections—and half-recoils from it, prizing the solidity and gratification of his home life, conscious of how it protects and supports him in the work that is the foundation of his identity. Half of him wants to gad about and learn to be a London insider; the other half wants to stay home, cook dinner, and write. As Lady M's pursuit heats up, his view of her goes from admiration, to criticism, to vicious condemnation.

One afternoon Lady Max takes Theroux home with her and tries to seduce him in her drawing room. She has just gotten him to kiss her when her daughter comes home unexpectedly; she screams at the girl for intruding and sends her upstairs. But the mood is broken. Lady Max lights a cigarette. Then:

> She was a heavy smoker and I was sitting near her. It was the odor of her lungs—not a rancid thing in her mouth, deeper. It seemed especially odd and offensive because she was so lovely. She had stubbed out her cigarette but she smelled strongly of smoke, of black, clammy London, of sooty air and stale breath. . . . She stank.

Theroux has turned on Lady Max, who is now identified in his mind with the grimy urban landscape. It is almost as if he were the protagonist in a Christian allegory, an innocent who, ashamed of his weakness, struggles against it, and allows himself to be partially seduced by the Devil in the form of a beautiful woman. Lovely on the outside, rotten within, she gets him into her clutches by showing him the city's secret places and garnering attention for his work, and almost succeeds in snatching his soul, but not quite.

The next time she phones, trying to get Theroux to take her to Brighton, which he's writing a piece on for a travel magazine (thanks to her), he pretends that his wife is going with him, remarking to the reader: "She was making me lie. I hated her for that most of all." But one has to ask: *was* Lady Max making him lie? Couldn't he have told her that he wasn't available for the kind of relationship she had in mind? Could he not have said that he wanted to be left alone to make his way by himself? Not speaking up has gotten Theroux into trouble before. The structure of the situation is like the one between him and Naipaul when Theroux can't make himself say anything about the taxi fares and the bill for lunch, or like the one between him and Birdie, or between him and Harry Lazard. Driven by his need for approval and belonging, he wants to be accepted and known by the world and can't resist when the world comes calling, even when it becomes important to do so to protect himself.

You have to sympathize with Theroux: he's alone all day, working hard to support his family, and knows scarcely anyone in London; he yearns to have his work recognized, and yearns to be wanted for who he is. Who among us doesn't desire these things? Yet at the same time, he sees himself as too much the injured party. "You pretend to be so innocent," Harry Lazard's wife had said when she tried to seduce him, and she had a point.

Theroux winds up as the object of unwanted attentions from older women with some regularity. It has happened at Moyo, with the nurse; in Singapore, with Fayette Lazard; it's happening in London, with Lady Max; and it happens in more than one of the chapters that follow. Apparently, Theroux needs to see himself as a man women lust after, women who are repulsive to him and to whom he's always superior. He has a habit of welcoming the attentions of powerful people—Vidia, Harry Lazard, Lady Max—and resenting these people when they expect something in return. He is too polite, and too fearful, to extricate himself from awkward situations by telling the truth and falls repeatedly into the role of one more sinned against than sinning. Theroux invites the reader to bear witness to, and sympathize with, his exploitation by powerful others. And speaking for myself, I'm all too ready to comply;

it feels familiar and comfortable to be on the side of an innocent and deserving aspirant to stardom taken advantage of by moral inferiors. Here he is, a devoted husband and father, working hard to support a family on the income from his writing, without an independent income or the valuable connections that could help his career, faultless, like the hero of a bildungsroman, taken advantage of by those with more power, more money, and bigger reputations. How can we not sympathize?

After he has turned against her, Theroux begins to do research on Lady Max. He has lunch with an American poet and longtime London resident whose book he's just reviewed and asks him if he knows her.

> "Oh, God," Bellamy said. He gave me a twisted smile of disgust. . . .
> "One had a thing—years ago, when one first came to London and was being introduced, as it were. When one was impressionable. When one was a bit dazzled, because one knew ever so much less."

Theroux's imitation of a certain British way of talking that the American poet has taken up is wonderful. Note that he has Bellamy represent himself as a hapless victim of Lady Max's wiles, "impressionable" and "dazzled," but Theroux, as a character in his own story, is shaken by the idea that he is not the first to have been pursued by the Lady. His amour propre is injured. Still, this is nothing compared to what he learns when he runs across his old pal Musprat at the London Library. They go for tea, and Theroux asks him point-blank his opinion of Lady Max. When he first met her, the poet says, Lady Max had mocked him, but after he'd won the Hawthornden Prize, she remembered his name and was nice. "'She's been to bed with everyone,' he said. 'Didn't you know that?'" Then, naming names, they make their way through a list of editors, poets, producers, novelists, museum directors, and journalists who have, according to Musprat, "had a leg over her." Many of them are the same people who have given Paul work and advanced his reputation.

Theroux doesn't comment on any of this, but when Lady Max surprises him by showing up at his house one afternoon in a taxi—it will be their last encounter—the way he writes about her lets us know the nature of his reaction.

> As she passed me on her way into the sitting room—she had not waited to be asked—I had a sense of other men on her, and I recalled how the bronze shell of the turtle door knocker at her house was stained black with fingerprints, all the men who had entered.

He's having his revenge.

I have to admit that the first time I read this chapter I was on Theroux's side. I saw Lady Max as beautiful, witty, sophisticated, and radiating allure. Then, as Theroux intended, I began to see her cruelty, her snobbery, her manipulativeness, and to resent the way she pressed herself on him, expecting to be rewarded for her attentions. And so when Bellamy and Musprat delivered their damning verdicts, and Theroux his damning comments, quoted above, I took them to be appropriate and deserved.

But the second time through I had to ask: why does Theroux make this woman so repellent? He's not an infant, after all. He would have been in his late thirties at the time he's writing about and in his fifties at the time he's writing this chapter. When he discovers Lady Max's many dalliances, why does he turn on her so viciously? And why does he choose to emphasize her promiscuity above all? This is the same man who tells us with more than a hint of pride, in the second chapter of *Sir Vidia's Shadow,* that he has slept with countless African women—guiltlessly—enjoying every minute; the sex is part of his daily routine. So what's happening in the Lady Max chapter is classic misogyny. It's all right for him to sleep around, but not for her.

Theroux treats his wife very well in *My Other Life,* in *Sir Vidia's Shadow,* and elsewhere. She comes across as a truth-teller with a tart tongue. But other women? In the scene where he rebuffs the advances of Fayette Lazard, she's reclining on a *chaise longue* dressed in a sarong, and at one point he refers to catching a glimpse of "the dark tarantula of her private parts." Where did that come from? When she touches him, Theroux writes, "I could feel the greed trembling in her bony fingers." Almost a comic-book description. Can it be a coincidence that when, in *Sir Vidia's Shadow,* Theroux introduces us to Vidia's second wife, who has offended him, she shares some of the same characteristics as Fayette and Lady Max? Overbearing, devious, grasping: she as spider, Vidia as fly.

I was in Florida while reading and writing about *My Other Life,* and when we met for lunch at the French bakery Maggie and I returned more than once to the subject of Theroux's treatment of women. We were offended. Maggie was inclined to write him off as a hopeless misogynist, but I wanted to see if we could understand a bit more about him. We forced ourselves to look at his behavior from a historical perspective. Theroux came of age before women's liberation; he went to college before feminism took hold in the academy. He spent a lot of time in England, a country not progressive in its attitudes toward women, and lived in places like Uganda, where, from a European-American perspective, attitudes were considerably worse. His writing doesn't display much familiarity with modern psychology—he never uses psychological concepts to interpret people's behavior, or to analyze his own. His gift is for dramatization, not analysis. But, though we had no hard evidence for this, we couldn't help feeling that, in addition to being culturally determined, Theroux's attitude toward women, and his ugly treatment of older women in particular, must have roots in his personal history.

Maggie and I agreed that the trouble had to have begun with his mother, but there was no way to find out more about it. Before *My Other Life,* Theroux had written another novel/memoir called *My Secret History,* not as riveting or well-crafted, which offered little in the way of clues. A long chapter on his experience as an altar boy in Medford, Massachusetts, and another on the time he spent teaching in Africa that fills in the circumstances of his sex life—even more active than I had gathered from *Sir Vidia's Shadow*—offered almost nothing to go on. For all that he writes about himself, Theroux avoids telling his readers anything that would help them understand him better.

I wanted to like Theroux, not get on his case. I'd wanted to know more about him because his relationship with Naipaul had struck deep chords in me. I was beginning to feel toward him the way I do toward a friend who acts badly from time to time but whom I forgive because he's my friend. I couldn't just dismiss him. And now, I was identifying not with but against him. The split between the good Theroux (the intelligent, observant dramatist of his own experience) and the bad Theroux (the man who behaved shabbily toward women) had taken shape in my mind. Why does Theroux treat the women in his work the way he does? I still didn't have an answer to that question, but, in place of an answer, memories of my own behavior toward men began coming back to me, unbidden.

I remembered a blind date I'd gone on in graduate school with a man who was involved in the theater, a big, burly man with intense black eyes, a swaggering manner, and black hair that had started to thin—he was older than me by quite a bit. At the end of the evening we pulled up in front of the house where I lived and suddenly his arms were around me, his face coming toward mine. When I pulled away, first gently, then with determination, he grew disgusted, and after it became clear I was having none of it, he said in a voice brimming with venom: "colder than an icicle on a witch's tit." The words hit me like a punch in the stomach. Stunned, I made my escape. The next day I discovered I'd lost an earring and knew it must have come off in his car—it belonged to a pair of antique pearl earrings my parents had given me. I phoned him and asked for it back. He refused, letting me know he was keeping it as punishment for *my* refusal. This man had had no right to expect me to kiss him at the end of a first date, especially since we'd had no special rapport. And his refusal to return the earring was mean and vindictive. Still, the incident troubled me.

Then another memory appeared. Again it was graduate school, and another burly man with a barrel chest and hulking shoulders, also older than me, an Indian post-doc in one of the sciences who invited me to dinner in his apartment. The first thing I saw when I came in was a table covered with groceries, and behind it, a cockroach halfway up the wall. We ate dinner; it was nice of him to have prepared it for me. We talked, he seemed a decent person; his being Indian was a novelty that made it interesting. Then somehow we were in the bedroom and suddenly the lights went out and his arms were around me. I was surprised and scared: I hadn't anticipated this, he'd seemed so nice. In the struggle I protested that he was married—he'd told me this earlier—and he said in my ear in his deep voice while he held me: "maddages ahd addainged in Indya, you know." I wanted to laugh and I felt sorry for him and was frightened all at the same time, but he let me go. The lights came back on. He was a decent man, as naïve in his way as I was in mine.

And then another incident came back and another, and in all of them I'd become entangled with a man whose designs I was unaware of, or didn't want to be aware of. The circumstances were different from Theroux's—I was in my early twenties and very inexperienced, I hadn't meant to be a tease or to arouse expectations—but at some level, it seemed to me I'd done the same thing Theroux had done with Birdie, and Lady Max, perhaps even with Fayette Lazard, and with other women he writes about later in the book: I'd let a man think I was interested in him, not realizing what I was doing. Even though I'd acted in ignorance, this was not something I could think poorly of someone else for getting into. In some way Theroux and I were alike, the common element being a mixture of ignorance and narcissism.

I'm not trying to find excuses for Theroux or to condone his objectionable behavior. But I'd like to refrain from judging him for it. There's lots of room for slippage in these situations, ambivalent feelings, mixed motives, conflicting signals. It's easy to make a mistake. It's no accident that, involuntarily, I kept remembering incidents I hadn't thought of in decades that showed me doing something akin to what he did. Though I judged myself at first, eventually I came to see that the incidents were comic, and that it was almost a matter of course that they'd occurred, given my scant knowledge of men, and of myself, at that age. It was obvious Theroux had problems where women were concerned—I was sure about that—and I didn't harbor any corresponding hostility toward men, as far as I knew, but I was more like Theroux than I'd imagined.

About a year after I'd finished *My Other Life,* I read a book that made my relation to it a lot clearer. The book was Peter Mayle's *A Year in Provence.* I read Mayle's book in preparation for a trip to the South of France, enjoying it all the more since a flare-up of my illness kept me from being able to write or cook or take a walk or do anything but lie there and read. Propped on a sofa in front of the fire on chilly June afternoons in the Catskills, fighting the growing realization that I wasn't going to be able to go on that trip after all, I was grateful to have so delicious a way to pass the time. When I finally canceled the ticket—for which there was no refund—I was bitterly disappointed, but the book went a long way toward making up for the loss.

It was pleasant being with Peter Mayle, a knowledgeable, witty, undemanding fellow; I could imagine the old stone walls, the garden, and the orchard of the house he and his wife were renovating, picture the two of them shopping at the local market, taste the bread, the olives, the fruit they ate, savor the wine they drank, enjoy hearing about the local craftsmen they met and the walks they took in the hills. It was a pastoral idyll set in a beautiful foreign place I'd probably never see.

But while Mayle's book offered me companionship, appeals to the senses, and mildly interesting information, it had none of the depth of Theroux's writing. Nobody changes in *A Year in Provence;* not much is at stake. It relies for its success on the reader's desire for a pleasurable, untroubled existence and, far from asking us to examine our lifestyle or values, it fulfills every upper-middle-class vacation fantasy. But the contrast revealed something else as well. It made me see that I had been developing with Theroux the kind of relationship—familiar to me from my reading life—that *A Year in Provence* provides, one geared entirely to my own needs. It guaranteed I could spend time with the author pleasantly and not be afraid he would put me off by his behavior or opinions. I'd been using Theroux, as I had used other authors—Alden Jones, Alain de Botton, and Rory Stewart, for instance—as a way to extend my experience beyond what the confines of my illness allowed, used them as guides to places I would probably never visit and experiences I would never have. I was counting on Theroux to do the same, and if he failed, well, he'd have to pay the penalty: criticism. I realized now that my unease at the incidents involving Birdie, Amina, Fayette Lazard, and Lady Max had upset my ability to sail serenely through my adventure. I didn't want my pleasure disrupted by mistakes in judgment, character flaws, or lack of awareness on the part of my companion. I was grateful to Theroux for his insights and evocations and had been depending on him for entertainment and companionship. But if understanding was what I wanted and not just enjoyment, that would require a different attitude on my part. I would have to try harder to see him for himself and not for his usefulness to me. There was one chapter left that held out the promise of insight, a chapter called "The Half-Life." I had one more chance to get it right.

12

"The Half-Life"

Paul has returned to America after eighteen years in England. He's about to get divorced. And he's a wreck. One doesn't know how much of what he tells us in this chapter actually happened and how much is made up, but the emotions it expresses can't be faked. Theroux describes how he used public telephones to communicate with his wife and remembers each one with painful vividness—exactly which exit a phone booth was near on the turnpike, next to which fast-food place it stood, the specific content of the agony he experienced at each one: "I used the public phones in order to hide the memories. When would I ever again see that roadside phone in Connecticut? But the day I did I almost wept and my throat ached with sadness." Maybe the phone booths weren't a part of it, maybe they were. But the agony is real.

Theroux becomes a true exile for the first time in his life: "I didn't realize that in losing my wife I lost everything. . . . It was a secular form of damnation; a half-life, halving again every second in an almost perpetual diminishment." He feels that half of his very being is missing. He can't be with people. He hides, gives out false names, false occupations. He's full of shame and misery. He can't write. He can't find anything to do. He distracts himself from the excruciating pain of being alive by reducing his daily experience as far as possible to numbers: calorie intake at each meal, miles rowed on the rowing machine, days since he last saw Allison, number of pictures he owns. He shops, buying things he doesn't need or that he already has: "I shopped with the knowledge that I was trying to fill the void of my sadness with material objects, anything to divert me or make me happy. . . . I felt humiliated by the expense and the duplication."

I felt tremendous sympathy and compassion for Theroux. I had been through two divorces and thought he'd done an extraordinary job of communicating the utter hell of those experiences. His ways of fending off the pain and getting by differed from mine, but the feelings of loss, failure, and humiliation were the same. An imminent divorce provides Theroux with some perspective on himself. He comes into possession of a few grains of wisdom (as did I). For the first time, he sees he isn't special, that his innermost experience is the same that other people have. He discovers that country music expresses exactly what he's feeling. Theroux's newfound humility endeared him to me. I knew whereof he spoke. Divorce brings your stock down to zero, but you go on living, like Melville's Ahab, with half a heart and half a lung.

The halfness of Theroux's life resonated with me in more ways than one. I lead a half-life, too. While other people my age are going to the gym, attending meetings, traveling, seeing plays, and visiting museums, I'm lying on the sofa, reading. Some days, getting up, eating breakfast, taking a shower, and getting dressed are enough to wear me out, and I have to lie down. Some days I can do one thing—have lunch with a friend or go to the movies. Some days I need complete rest. On other days I can do two things, once in a while three. At times I hire people to grocery-shop and run errands; at times I do those things myself. A visit from a computer technician can use up my energy for the rest of the day. Having lived like this for many years, most of the time I no longer feel deprived. My half-life feels whole, as long as I'm alert enough to appreciate the goodness of what I have. What is half and what is whole are relative. Some days, my life is fuller and more delectable than it ever was before. Theroux, on the other hand, suffering the agonies of a separation leading to divorce, is in misery's grip.

Attempting to alleviate the anguish, he goes to a psychiatrist, looking, as he puts it, "for uncritical and anonymous company." Theroux has assigned his psychiatrist the role of someone who can fulfill his needs in a pleasant, undemanding way, rather like a good servant. "Fortunately," he adds, "she was good-looking." An alarm bell went off when I read that, but I decided to overlook it. At first, Theroux tells us, the only things he lied about were his name and occupation. Pavel Medved, particle physicist. Another alarm bell—lying to his therapist right off the bat—how does he expect her to be able to help him? Perhaps the unfamiliar situation made him afraid. Theroux is uncomfortable in his role as patient, complains of being forced to carry the conversational ball and of not liking to talk about himself because he's not used to it. Gradually, his discomfort turns to hostility. One day, while talking about how miserable he feels, he cries out to the therapist—her name is Dr. Mylchreest—"'How can you analyze it? I feel like shit.' I had begun shouting, 'Can you imagine analyzing shit?'"

> I lowered my voice, and I was aware that I was paying this woman to listen to me. It made me self-conscious and unwilling. I understood the impotence some men experience with a prostitute when they are up in her room and, after she has counted the money, she opens her legs.

What? Suddenly the therapist has become "this woman," a woman he compares to a prostitute. Though I knew better, I thought it possible that the analogy might be random. I'd wait and see. I didn't have to wait long. Besides having to pay her to listen to him, one of the things Theroux resents about his therapist is the time limit she places on his visits. He feels she's treating him coldly when she reminds him that time is up.

> "Your time is up," she said, and she had never looked prettier to me, though I could only think that she was waiting there for the next man, like a hooker in a room turning tricks.

Prostitution again. I begin to wonder: can Theroux encounter any woman not his wife who doesn't arouse feelings of anger and contempt? The reaction seems unconscious; he's completely unaware that his attitude toward women is demeaning; his behavior is reflexive and beyond his control.

His relationship to Dr. Mylchreest becomes increasingly manipulative. The lies multiply. He falls in love with her.

> I knew it would frighten her if I told her how I felt, and so I concealed my feelings towards her, but in the sessions after this I talked about sex—dreams, impulses, episodes from the past, many of them invented. A common theme was that I was highly charged sexually and that my marriage had been awkward as a result—my wife unwilling.

The baldness of this attempt to seduce his therapist by emphasizing his sexual energy is equaled in its transparency only by his attempt to win her over by showing how much he knows about Freud, and then, for good measure, boasting about the art he owns, the languages he speaks, the places he's been. Then, sensing that this is getting him nowhere, he changes tactics and relates a recurring dream in which he is complicit in the murder of someone—a woman—whose body is chopped up and put in a suitcase. He helps her murderers to dispose of the suitcase and they escape. After Theroux has declared his love and has been informed that falling in love with the therapist is something that regularly occurs in the psychotherapeutic process, he reveals to Dr. Mylchreest that it is she who was in the suitcase and warns that he may become disillusioned and try to hurt her.

At their last session — Theroux's behavior has made it impossible to continue — Dr. Mylchreest gives him a four-page reading list that happens to contain several of his novels. Theroux questions Dr. Mylchreest closely as to what she expects him to get from reading these books; she replies neutrally that she believes they might supply him with suggestions and possibilities but makes no further claims. Theroux can't decide whether or not she knows who he is. Since he's leaving after little more than a month of treatment, Theroux feels he has to justify himself to the reader, saying that it was "the writer" in him that dictated his departure: "that was the great thing about being a writer in therapy — of course you failed, because you needed your secrets but you always had the last word." I don't know what he means by needing his secrets, but Theroux appears to take comfort in the idea that he can have the last word by writing about the experience. Apparently, he needs to feel that he's gotten the upper hand.

Theroux's ignorance of himself and of the situation he's in is painful. He thinks he's brought his relationship with Dr. Mylchreest to a satisfactory conclusion; in fact, what could have been a step toward understanding his life and cleaning up his act has been used as a stop-gap measure to boost his ego, dissipate his loneliness, and provide an outlet for his anger. He decides that the solution to the misery he feels at being separated from his wife is to write: "then I would recover my missing self." His talent is what will save him, not the ministrations of some woman.

Theroux is desperate. He's lost his wife; his relations with his sons will never be the same; he will never again have the domestic happiness he's written about with such fervor; he hasn't been able to function socially or professionally. His viability as a human being seems in question. If the only way he can reconstitute himself is to return to old habits—using writing as a refuge and a weapon, asserting his male superiority—then that is what he must do. Two years later Theroux will come to the same decision on the Gloucester Road after receiving Vidia's rejection: his first thought is to write a book about it. Writing is his way of dealing with the devastations of experience; it's an outlet that can soothe and contain raw feelings, a device for sorting his thoughts, reducing the chaos, producing an account of things that makes some kind of sense.

Theroux is only doing what human beings do: when threatened, we rely on our defenses, strategies devised long ago to shield us from the world. The character Theroux portrays here as himself is too shell-shocked and vulnerable to respond to psychotherapy, which presents him with an unfamiliar and threatening situation. The power distribution is too unequal. He must reveal everything, while the therapist—a woman, no less—reveals nothing. So he lies. And then he exits. To give him credit, Theroux describes the therapist as behaving in a professional manner: she's skillful, judicious, and well-intentioned; she never flirts. As a character, fictional or not, Dr. Mylchreest is believable to anyone who's ever been in Freudian therapy. But having thus characterized her, when Theroux, not once but twice, compares her to a whore, using language like "turning tricks" and "opening her legs," the reaction makes no sense. It's clear he feels seriously threatened by Dr. Mylchreest and strikes out in self-defense, but the person he's attacking is not his therapist but someone who had hurt him long ago. When I recognized this, it changed my attitude toward him. I got over being angry with Theroux for comparing his therapist to a prostitute and for throwing away the chance to learn about himself. Something in his past produced these reactions;

he's acting not from choice but from reflex. And then, right on schedule, I began to have memories of my own first sessions with a psychotherapist.

Because I'd been in therapy many times since, I'd forgotten how ignorant I was at first, how unable to make head or tail of what was going on. I had left my first husband and was living with a lover in a nearby city, frightened to death of what I was doing. The tall young man with spectacles and a solemn air to whom I had turned for guidance made me feel out of my depth. He expected me to talk about myself, which, like Theroux, I wasn't used to doing, at least not in the terms expected of me as I sat facing him in his small, underheated office. With his long face and sober expression, he, like Dr. Mylchreest, was strangely impersonal, and when he announced at the end of the first few sessions that our time was up, I thought he didn't care whether I lived or died.

Like Theroux, I was at sea in my life, trying to stay afloat by enlisting the help of a paid professional with an unfamiliar vocabulary and the air of one who possesses secret knowledge. Only in my case it was someone whose judgments I feared, and whom I wished to please, as I wished to please all figures of authority. Though the bespectacled young man meant well—I think I must have been among his earliest patients—he did not in the end help me to understand myself much better than when I started. But I did come to recognize that I had lived my life with virtually no consciousness of my emotions. I *had* emotions, that was certain, more than my share, but I was not in the habit of noticing them, much less of making them into objects of analysis. Emotions were not high on my list of things to pay attention to—it was the intellect that mattered, wasn't it?—that was what my whole life had taught me up to that point. I was in a highly competitive graduate program, struggling to stay afloat, and this new awareness of my feelings didn't promise to take me very far in that en-

terprise, so, having no reinforcements on any side, the awareness
languished.

One thing the young man told me, which I refused to believe
at the time though I had a suspicion it might be true, was that my
affair with the man I had left my husband for wouldn't save me.
He was right about that—it nearly destroyed me—but it was the
making of me, too. When I left him, my lover, who turned out to
be an alcoholic, got me fired from my job at the school where we
both taught. For the first time in my life I suffered consciously and
intensely and at length. And even as I did so, months later, walking the streets of Philadelphia, where I had managed to get another job, looking as if I had seen a ghost, and wondering whether
I were going to survive, like Theroux, I knew that I had finally
joined the human race.

So I had to let up on Theroux. I hadn't done much better in
my first encounter with psychotherapy than he had. My ignorance had a different shape from his—I didn't deceive or threaten
my doctor; on the contrary, I wanted to perform well and be a
good pupil—but I was just as clueless and, if anything, even more
ignorant of myself. How ignorant, it shocks me to think of now.
And, much later in life, when I got sick, like Theroux at the time
of his divorce and after the breakup with Vidia, I resorted to a
familiar means of salving my pain: he wrote, I read. We both fell
back on old defenses. I finally saw that there was no percentage
in criticizing this man whom, all along, I had very much liked.
He may have had problems in his relationships with women that
caused him to treat them unfairly, but who doesn't have problems
that have a negative effect on others? Because I'd experienced
gender discrimination, I was bound to land on Theroux for his
misogyny. It was low-hanging fruit. But I no longer felt the need
to get on his case for it. It came to me—again, like clockwork—
that should I decide to turn my attention to the way in which I'd
left both my first and second husbands, there would be little to

choose between us where hurting other people was concerned. After I left, my first husband told me that he gave a rope that was in our apartment to a neighbor so that he wouldn't use it to hang himself. I had never anticipated anything like that, but then, I hadn't thought much about it, either.

13

Henning Mankell

So much self-scrutiny was abrading. I needed a break, a break from Naipaul and Theroux and a vacation from self-analysis. The novels of Henning Mankell attracted me powerfully. It would be a relief to plunge into mysteries set in a foreign country—in this case, Sweden—in the company of Mankell's depressive main character, Kurt Wallander, whom I loved spending time with, though I didn't know why. It didn't matter. I wanted to get lost.

Kurt Wallander is a middle-aged detective inspector who's been on the force for some twenty-five or thirty years. Divorced, with one daughter, he lives alone in Ystad, a city in the province of Skåne on the southern coast of Sweden, a town that, if you believe the author, has some of the worst weather in world, and little else to recommend it. Wallander has no friends to speak of—his coworkers are as close as he comes—and no hobbies other than listening to opera on tapes. His work is his life. He spends all his time hunting down people who commit murder—a job he finds difficult, frustrating, and exhausting. It sounds grim, and it is.

In reading *My Other Life,* although I'd had my problems with him, I had sympathized with Theroux—Theroux the author and Theroux the character he's writing about—liked him, felt close to him, went through what he was going through. With Henning Mankell that relationship—identifying with a narrator and the literary character he's depicting—became something more. Not only do I sympathize with Mankell/Wallander and undergo his experiences as if they were my own, I'm so identified with him that comparing his experience to mine feels redundant. There's no space between Wallander and me. In figuring out what was going on with this man, I would automatically be discovering something about myself. This, despite my knowing that in most external, tangible ways I was nothing like the middle-aged Swedish detective or his author—to whom I'd turned, ironically, for escape.

Nor can I be the only person for whom this is true. The Kurt Wallander novels have been popular all over the world for more than twenty years, and their appeal doesn't stem from any of the usual sources. There's no sex, not much violence compared to most mystery novels, no fast living, hot cars, exotic locales, beautiful women, gorgeous clothes, or luxury hotels. You don't feel you're getting the inside story on corporations, governments, industries, professions, arcane fields of knowledge, technology, or any of the latest trends. In other words, there are no appeals to the desire to be cool or in the know, to pride, lust, fame, greed, or the senses. There are temptations here, but they're not self-evident. It's a harsh, gray, uncomfortable, monotonous world. So what can be the appeal? Here's a typical passage from a novel called *One Step Behind*. Wallander is speaking to a colleague—they're sitting in some nondescript café. Wallander asks Nyberg if he wants more coffee, and Nyberg declines.

> "I have more than 20 cups a day," he said. "To keep my energy up. Actually, maybe just to keep going."
>
> "Police work wouldn't be possible without coffee," Wallander said.
>
> "No work would be possible without coffee."
>
> They pondered the importance of coffee in silence. Some people at a nearby table got up and left.

The characters' pronouncements about coffee are so solemn, you can't help smiling. What they say about coffee is certainly true for them: Wallander consumes an enormous amount of it, and though excessive coffee-drinking figures in other Swedish mystery series, it seems to reach outrageous proportions here. Wallander uses coffee to force himself to stay awake. In the novel's opening scene, he falls asleep at the wheel of his old Peugeot and narrowly escapes getting killed. In the final pages, he confronts the murderer after not having slept for more than twenty-four hours. We wish desperately that he would get more sleep.

Coffee aside, this passage is Mankell's style at its frugal best. Not an extra syllable. The style, like Wallander, is taciturn, withholding, and dour. Also straightforward and matter-of-fact: "No work would be possible without coffee." Mankell's characters' speech is parsimonious, as if the slightest suggestion of ornamentation or volubility would convict them of a crime. Those would be the crimes of falsehood (prettying up the facts), frivolity (focusing on the merely decorative or pleasing), and waste (spending time and energy on the inessential). If this seems exaggerated, think again. The more one reads of Wallander and his ways, the more clear it is that beneath his Puritanical resistance to the art of expression, and the inclination to withhold thoughts rather than to speak them, lies a belief that in the face of the harshness of existence, silence is the safest, and indeed the only proper, response. These characters' inability, or unwillingness, to speak suggests that there's no point in it. They speak the language of persons who, like the singer in "Ol' Man River," are "weary and sick of trying." The question is, how can writing that in so many ways radiates depression give so much pleasure?

Let's look more closely. At the very end of the passage quoted above, Mankell writes: "Some people at a nearby table got up and left." The sentence puts period to the preceding dialogue and shares with it the qualities of plainness and thrift. The departure of the people makes some kind of oblique comment on what has just occurred, but what the comment is, we don't know. The *thereness* of a sentence like this, the simple fact recorded with no attempt at explanation, contains the essence of Mankell's world. It suggests something like this: don't editorialize, don't look for hidden meanings, and above all don't *add* anything to what's in front of you. What is just is, so leave it alone. "Some people at a nearby table got up and left." End of story. And yet, it's as if, with sentences like this, scattered throughout the Wallander novels, Mankell were expressing the desire that there *should* be more to life and valiantly suppressing it at the same time.

One can speculate about the function of such a sentence in a work of suspense. Sometimes mystery writers drop into the narrative bits of information that seem trivial at the time but assume great importance later on; it's a way of providing clues — some false, some true — that give the reader a chance to solve the mystery before the detectives do. The sentence about the people who got up and left could be one of these. Or, by strewing these factual statements at intervals throughout the narrative, Mankell may simply be giving it body, anchoring a scene in place, conferring reality upon a moment by pinning it down with a detail. And so he is. But that's not all there is to it. Such sentences support the worldview implied by the sparse and slightly dogged quality of his prose, insisting on the untranscendable *thereness* of things. And yet, behind their willful assertion that that's all there is, lurks the wisp of a wish that it weren't so.

Kurt Wallander is an extension of the outlook on life that Mankell's language implies, a man who plods through the day, day after day, exhausted, discouraged, encountering blows to his psyche, to his theories about the case, to his vacation plans, but who continues, rain or shine, to put one foot in front of the other. At a certain point in *One Step Behind* (a title that echoes this perspective) he spills coffee on himself and goes around for most of the day with a large stain on his shirt because there's no time to go back to his apartment and change. The stain might stand for all the punishment Wallander puts up with as he bulldogs his way through a case, punishment for which he himself is sometimes responsible. This is why I love him. He's not a whiz-bang hero like James Bond, he has no supernatural abilities, he isn't drop-dead handsome, not a crusader for justice or a genius at detection; though intelligent and persevering, he's not outstanding in any way that you can put your finger on, and yet, when it comes to finding a murderer, you wouldn't trade him for anybody else. His luck isn't that good, he eats bad food, drinks too much, misses doctor's appointments, doesn't live up to his best intentions, drives himself mercilessly, falls down, and keeps on going. The suffering, the moral failures, the ordinariness, draw him close. This man is no better than ourselves.

Yet though I feel close to Wallander, I don't know him very well. He's not introspective. We don't know much about his formative years. He's reflective: ponders the facts of his cases obsessively, wonders about the people he interviews, worries about his daughter, contemplates, glumly, the government's diminishing support for police work, and is disturbed by the increasing social disintegration in his country. Wallander thinks about these and other issues, but he doesn't think much about himself. Sometimes I want to shake him and say, wake up, Kurt, go to the doctor, change your diet, get more sleep, go to the movies, go see one of those operas you love so much—Wallander loves to listen to opera recordings, but never once in the books I've read does he ever *go* to the opera—call your daughter, ask yourself why you don't have any friends, move out of that apartment on Mariagatan into a place that would give you some pleasure. Live before you die. In some ways being with Kurt Wallander is like being with someone you love: you can see how they cause themselves pain, but pointing it out doesn't do any good.

I've said Wallander is not introspective, but there's an exception to this. In *The Man Who Smiled,* I noticed, at several points he pauses to criticize himself for something he's done, or, more likely, hasn't done. It ranges from something as small as "he should have put on a thicker jacket," to "I'm a man who doesn't laugh enough," to blaming himself for a murder victim's death because he'd been too depressed to recognize a genuine plea for help. Wallander blames himself a lot, and often his self-criticisms are just. But they rarely lead anywhere. They spring from a habit of self-deprecation rather than from a desire for change. And this, too, makes him easy to identify with. He wants to be better, but at a deep level, he lacks the motivation, or perhaps the belief that change is possible. Wallander's refusal to accept compliments for his outstanding police work is of a piece with his reflexive self-criticism. He ungraciously sweeps aside all praise for his achievements, proudly sticking to his low opinion of himself: nobody is going to take that away from him. He doesn't see that gruffly turning away a compliment is like shoving a gift down the giver's throat instead of recognizing it for the well-meant gesture that it is.

The sadness that surrounds Wallander comes from his inability to receive joy and pleasure. He doesn't notice the beauty in his surroundings. Trees, forests, meadows, gardens produce no effect on him. He likes the ocean and open fields but uses them mainly as places to walk off his worries or to think about a case. He doesn't enjoy his food. He's always so exhausted that rest and sleep, rather than being pleasurable, are only ways to forestall collapse. He's sensitive to the weather, which in Skåne consists mainly of rain, snow, wind, and increasing cold—how many times does he turn up his collar and clutch his coat about him, shivering?—but even when the weather is fine he isn't gladdened by it. The summer is always too hot. In *The White Lioness,* having been up for most of the night, he goes home, eats a couple of stale rolls, drinks a beer, and falls asleep in his clothes. The next morning he's at the station at seven thirty. After an eight o'clock meeting, he steps outside on his way somewhere and Mankell writes: "Wallander went out to his car. It was going to be a nice day in Skåne. He paused and filled his lungs with air." There's no indication that he enjoyed taking this breath; we have to infer it. Mankell is afraid to register pleasure on his character's behalf. He'll allow Wallander to stare at the ocean from time to time but will never say what it did for his spirit, won't tell us whether or not his hero enjoyed that late-night beer. Does Mankell believe that seeking pleasure, or acknowledging that one has experienced it, is a sign of weakness or self-indulgence? It would seem so.

At times Wallander is unable even to be nourished by food, much less to enjoy it. It's as if he has no connection to it, can't fit it into his life. Once, after informing a husband that his wife, missing for several days, has been found dead, he stops on the highway for a bite. He "struggled to eat a hamburger. He couldn't remember when he had last eaten. Then he hurried to the police station." Eating is a struggle squeezed in between unpleasant duties and often forgotten.

The stresses associated with his job are so great that normal activities—drink, food, rest, sleep, taking a deep breath—are robbed of their nutritive value. Like coffee, they're undertaken for the sole purpose of keeping him going; he lives to work. Nothing matters but the case.

While Wallander's sensory experience—eating, drinking, sleeping—gives him no pleasure and often involves discomfort, its role in the reader's relation to the novels is crucial. Mankell's registry of the physical world his characters inhabit grounds his readers continually in time and space and binds us to the protagonist with constant reminders of his bodily existence. The fact that his sensations are mostly unpleasant makes them all the more real. There are the light touches—"Wallander took a sip of cold coffee before going on"—and the details that make a place and a moment believable—"They sat there in silence. Somebody in the corridor was complaining that the coffee machine was broken." The cold coffee, the complaining people, and the broken machine typify what I've come to think of as the downhill direction of Wallander's observations, which often tally with our own experience. When you take a sip of coffee before continuing to speak in a meeting, it's likely to be cold.

Mankell garners our trust by repeatedly observing the unsatisfactory nature of experience, one form of which is frustration. Coming up against brick walls in the solving of a case is standard in crime fiction, but it's Wallander's small daily frustrations that touch us where we live: "He took two wrong turns before he reached the correct address." "He tried to think what it was about his father that reminded him of himself. But he could not find the answer." When Wallander buys a Christmas tree, no matter how thoroughly he scours his apartment, he can't find the stand for it; later, when he comes home from shopping for all the things he hasn't bought over the last several months, he realizes the stand is the one thing he's forgotten to get. How can you not believe in this man, how can you not be on his side?

Such details, distributed throughout Mankell's text, anchor us ever more firmly to the world he's created and bind us more closely to his protagonist, and they increase our desire that Wallander should succeed at something—whether it be tracking down a suspect, improved relations with his daughter, meeting someone—a woman—or just having a decent meal now and then. Every so often, Mankell gives us a large helping of these grounding details all at once:

He drove home and cooked a meal he would have been incapable of describing afterward. He watered the five plants he had on his window ledges, filled the washing machine with clothes that had been strewn around the apartment, discovered he had no laundry detergent, then sat on the sofa and cut his toenails. Occasionally he looked around the room, as if he expected to find that he wasn't alone after all. Shortly after 10:00 he went to bed and fell asleep almost immediately.

Outside the rain had eased off and become a light drizzle.

The passage doesn't advance the plot; it doesn't tell us anything about Wallander we don't already know, so why is it there? Is Mankell insisting on the prosaic, humdrum nature of human life? Maybe. In most fiction, popular or literary, it doesn't get much grittier than cutting your toenails. Is he continuing to develop Wallander's character? Wallander doesn't remember what he ate, he has no relationship to his plants (the only thing he notes about them is that there are "five"), he's a sloppy housekeeper who strews dirty clothes around the apartment and forgets to buy laundry soap, but none of this is new. Is he lonely? Wallander's surprise that there's no one else there implies that he's not feeling lonely on that particular evening. What, then? Perhaps this passage is a kind of lullaby. Wallander goes about feeding himself and putting his living space to rights. He grooms himself and goes to bed early. Apparently untroubled, he falls asleep immediately. And the rain, instead of coming down harder, eases off; for once, the wind is not even mentioned.

The gratuitousness of the paragraph is like that of the statement following Wallander and Nyberg's conversation about coffee: "Some people at a nearby table got up and left." It's ballast, giving weight to the world imagination has crafted. Still, I can't help feeling that, in addition, the passage is asking us to contemplate the sufficiency, and insufficiency, of these acts of maintaining the self in existence: cooking and eating, watering the plants, doing the laundry. As Mankell describes them they have the same faintly dispiriting air as the sentence about the people leaving the nearby table, as much as to say: "That's all there is. There isn't any more." Meanwhile, standing by itself on the page, and serving—just possibly—as a Skånian form of benediction intimating that all may yet be well, comes the sentence: "Outside the rain had eased off and become a light drizzle."

Philosophical questions aside, when it comes right down to it, I have to admit, I like Wallander's life exactly the way it is. It's murder, after all; the killer could strike again. I want Wallander to be out there protecting people from harm, not safe in his bed or preoccupied with cleaning up his apartment. He's a father figure: one who stays awake so that others can sleep, risks his life so that the rest of us can live, and is thoroughly convinced that it is he, and he alone, who must do these things. And, though I'm always wanting to tell him to go home, take the day off, have a good meal, kick back, and watch TV, I really don't want him to change, because I want his protection and because in another sense I *am* him. His self-destructive, compulsive behavior mirrors both the workaholic adult and the autistic child in me. I like it that he decides to drive to some godforsaken place in the north of Sweden before breakfast, that he gets up in the middle of the night to revisit a crime scene. I'm secretly happy when he forgets to visit his solitary, uncommunicative, and rather unpleasant father because work has forced everything else from his mind. It's satisfying to identify with someone who's going to triumph over evil through a combination of stubbornness, self-sacrifice, and courage. And, although I hate his going around with that stain on his shirt, there's a part of me that thinks, yes, that's just what's required. Like an old hammer or an old wrench, he's battered, worn down, and grimed by his experience, but he gets the job done, a bit beaten up, but, in a pinch, reliable, workmanlike, and effective.

Wallander's defects constitute his allure. I love his doggedness, one-track mind, and self-destructive habits. Yet the thing about him I find hardest to take follows directly from his one-pointed, task-obsessed mind-set: it's that often he doesn't treat people kindly, doesn't thank them enough for their help, or try to empathize with them. Not receiving their compliments is the least of it. Several times it occurs to him that he ought ask his coworker Ann-Britt Höglund how she is—he knows she's been going through a long and painful divorce—but he never does: he's too tired, too preoccupied with his job, basically, too self-involved, to take the trouble. He doesn't notice the effect he has on others. After one of his gruff exchanges I often imagine that he feels a remorse which he suppresses because he believes it's more important to keep on doing his work than to go back and make things right.

Wallander struggles in all the primary relationships of his life: with his wife, Mona, from whom he's divorced, with his father, the painter, who never forgave him for becoming a policeman, with his daughter, Linda, with whom things are always going from smooth to rocky and back again, with his girlfriend, Baiba, of whom he, and we, see very little. He carries these relationships with him through his workdays both as solace and as burden, chiefly the latter. At first, they seem incidental to the narrative, which tracks his attempts to piece together the evidences of crime. But as I read deeper into the series, I found myself more interested in Wallander's moods, problems, and habits—his desire to have a dog, live in the country, repair the relationship with his father—than in his catching the killer.

In a brief afterword he wrote to *An Event in Autumn,* Mankell says he believes the enormous popularity of the Wallander series is owing to the fact that "from the very beginning . . . I was clear that I would create a human being who was very like myself and the unknown reader." Mankell knew what he was doing. People respond to these novels because they can identify with the protagonist. He continues: "I also realized that I needed to be afraid of the character I had created. . . . There would always be a danger of my forgetting to write novels to be performed by a full orchestra, and instead to concentrate on his horn solos. What I needed always to bear in mind was: the story is the most important thing. Always." Mankell is reminding himself not to become so involved with Wallander—the horn solo—that he neglects the score for the full orchestra—the plot, the setting, the other characters, and the social issues he means to explore.

Mankell takes his own advice. Though now and then he may wind up a story a little too hastily, drop a stitch or two by planting an unbelievable clue, his plots are consistently complex, layered, and meticulously constructed; the pace at which they unfold is perfection. Often there's a significant social or political theme, such as immigration problems, involved. And most novels contain interesting minor characters whom we wish we could see more of. Each time I read a new novel, I'm completely immersed in the story, which holds my attention in a tight grip until the final moment. Yet despite my involvement in the warp and woof of every plot, when I think back over the novels it's only Wallander I remember.

In some way Wallander exemplifies the mystery of being alive. Like Theroux on his way to Patagonia, his life is shadowed by a never-formulated question: why live? He refuses to believe in any sort of overriding purpose, higher power, or spiritual reality that might rationalize or give point to existence. He makes skeptical, semi-sarcastic remarks about religion, exhibiting a secular mentality not willful or belligerent, but one that reflects the norm for people of his time and place. For Kurt, it wouldn't be honest to place his faith in anything beyond what he can see and touch. His work brings him into contact on a regular basis with such pain and horror, and its successful resolution depends so much on the careful tracking down of hard information, the fitting together of small pieces of physical evidence—an ashtray out of place, the opening of a sticky window—that he can't imagine what other form of redemption there might be. Besides, he doesn't have time. His faithfulness to the facts of the cases he investigates leads him to their successful conclusion and is the upside of his refusal to interpret the world in loftier terms. The solution substitutes for any larger meaning or purpose his life might have.

He plods, he hews to the facts, he keeps his nose to the grind-stone, but—and this came as a surprise to me when I realized it— he solves his cases as much by intuition as by deduction, obeying an instinct that tells him something is not quite right, or that there's something he's overlooked, or that he'd better go back and check some detail one more time. His mentor, Rydberg, whom he revered, had told him to pay attention to his hunches, and he does so, religiously. Almost always, the hunch pays off. For a materialist, he is curiously dependent on a sixth sense. Perhaps it's his refusal to search for meaning anywhere but in the facts before him that gives him the leeway occasionally to obey gut instinct. However that may be, by yielding to vagrant impulses and ghostly inklings in his search for the killer, Wallander, in effect, acknowledges his membership in the realm of sentient beings who operate on instinct, not ratiocination. In honoring this part of himself, which is both gut-level and supersensory at the same time, he becomes connected to the larger universe, a vast web of life he would never explicitly recognize but on whose existence he depends for the successful prosecution of his work, not least because it is to this larger whole that the killer belongs as well. Mankell is having it both ways: the world is all that is the case, but, it turns out, hunches and intuitions, impulses and inklings, are part of the world, a place that is joined to itself by connections invisible to the naked eye.

At the conscious level Wallander is an unaccommodated man. Without friends, without comforts physical or spiritual, with little in the way of reward, without respite and without rest, he pursues his object. The weather is bad, he's tired, and often just as unhappy with himself as with the progress of the case. He's depressed. Not so badly that he can't get up in the morning, not so badly that he can't formulate a plan and stick to it, more or less, but depressed in that he can't allow pleasure or joy to overtake him except in rare moments, and must drive himself ruthlessly in order to maintain a sense of his own integrity and value. Robbed of the solace that a spiritual life or a close family life or an avocation or a creative outlet might afford, he embraces a Protestant work ethic that is quasi-suicidal. He keeps going, while going without. This man's sadness cannot be plumbed, in part, because he can't even let himself know that it's there. His loneliness is unbreachable.

While people who are depressed can be hard to spend time with, being with them can also be a relief. They don't pretend about anything. They never knowingly lie. With them there's no need to keep up appearances—they can't do it, so why need we?—and when the need for it falls away, one suddenly becomes aware of the enormous effort involved in maintaining a cheerful façade. Maybe this is why I find Wallander so appealing. When I'm reading about him, I don't have to pretend—to myself—that everything's okay. It's a relief to be able to admit freely that you're feeling low and things aren't going well. When you can face it squarely, and then relax around it, depression diminishes in importance and loses some of its power. There's a comfort in simply acknowledging it: that comfort, I suspect, is the basis of my attraction to this character.

Once, long ago, Emily Dickinson played the same role for me

that Mankell does now. The first year I taught in Philadelphia I'd left my first husband, had had a disastrous (though thrilling) affair, and, after having done well at a topflight graduate school, was having trouble keeping my job at a third-tier university. I didn't become suicidal, but the option of simply not being alive presented itself. In such a mood, I noticed that when I read the poems of Emily Dickinson, I felt better. This was especially true of poems with first lines like "Good morning, Midnight, I'm coming home," and "One crucifixion is recorded only." The more pain the poem had in it, the better. I wondered about this. Why should Emily Dickinson's suffering have a salutary effect on me? Wasn't there something ghoulish in that? But the answer was simple: it comforted me to know that someone else had felt as much pain as I did and wasn't ashamed to write about it. Reading Dickinson made me feel less alone. So does reading Mankell. Because Mankell's novels feature a man who's struggling and frequently on the edge of depression, they let me know I'm not alone in whatever sadness or difficulties I may be experiencing. When I find myself halfway through a case with Wallander, I usually notice that my comfort level has risen. My inadequacies seem less glaring, I'm more at home in the world; his presence steadies me, his persistence is a source of strength.

Sometimes, though, Wallander's curmudgeonly refusal to be gladdened by anything lends an unnecessarily dismal cast to his experience: "He looked out the window. Some blackbirds were screeching over by the water tower. He tried to count them, but there were too many." A sight that might cause another person to become interested in the birds and energized by their excitement makes Wallander frustrated—he can't count them because there are "too many"—their "screeching" grates on him. Similarly, when he steps out of the station on his way somewhere and records his take on the weather, he notes: "The wind was still gusty, and now it had started to rain." First a disappointment—the wind is *still* gusty (it might have died down), and not only that, things have gotten worse—*now* it's started to rain. The negative direction of the observation is slight but definite. None of these sentences, by themselves, seem abnormally gloomy, but, over time, they add up. Wallander intensifies his bleak mood with perceptions that have been shaped by it in the first place; he exists inside a negative feedback loop that reinforces his discouragement.

Sometimes I see Wallander as our suffering servant, undergoing his trials so that we can perceive the ravages of our own lifestyle, glimpse the bleakness of our worldview, and the poverty of our relationships. Sometimes I see him as a secular saint, bowed down though never crushed by the soul-destroying nature of his work, pursued by the demons of remorse, not giving up. A stalwart man upon whom one can rely, a man who thinks first of his duty and rarely of himself. If I sound like Raymond Chandler describing Philip Marlowe, it's probably because the characters have a family resemblance—loners, beat up by life, who won't quit. But Wallander, unlike Marlowe, is not a cynic. Nor is he a moralist. He just notes, glumly, that things are going downhill. Wallander's experience functions for me, and perhaps for other readers, as a metaphor for the way life feels sometimes: long, hard, frustrating, unsatisfactory, and inescapable. It appears there's great solace in this, when one meets it in the pages of a book.

At the end of *The White Lioness* Wallander's drivenness catches up with him. He falls apart not when the pressure is greatest but when everything's over and he has time to rest, eat, sleep, and feel what's going on inside of him. When this happens, he has to go on extended medical leave and see a doctor twice a week—the cause, clinical depression. His colleagues fear he may never come back. But he does come back—Mankell gives an account of the depression and Wallander's emergence from it at the beginning of *The Man Who Smiled*. He resumes his responsibilities and continues very much as before. His persistent bad habits eventually

.

produce diabetes. Peripherally aware that he's ignoring crucial aspects of his life, he chooses, in the words of Conrad's Marlowe, who is the model for Chandler's, to be "faithful to the nightmare of his choice." He still cares about Linda, still visits his father at irregular intervals, but he never goes to the opera and most of the time simply forges ahead on the case he's working. He makes do with the portion he has chosen. This is where his heroism lies, and his crucifixion. He solves the case, yet what's missing, the thing that isn't there in his life, dogs him; the pain of it is beyond words, yet still he keeps going, living a life that both is and is not enough.

In the end, Wallander does buy a house in the country where he can potter in the garden, have a dog, and walk by the sea. There he entertains Linda, who now has a partner and an infant. But it is not long before the Alzheimer's that took his father starts its slow descent. There is no recourse, and no quarter given. In an end that follows from the logic of his life, everything is extinguished. In Wallander's final moments there will be no hand reaching down to take his in its grasp. Just a grave to receive his body. "Some people at a nearby table got up and left."

14

Envy, Love, and Writing

Mankell consigns Wallander to oblivion with no pronouncements about the meaning of his life or any other attempt to mitigate the impact of his death. One might think this would be hard to take, after reading all twelve books in the series, but it isn't. Mankell lets Wallander go with a kind of stoicism that is comforting in its refusal to offer comfort. No claims, no pretense, just acceptance. I found the title of Ann Patchett's essay collection *This Is the Story of a Happy Marriage* much more frightening, since it brought to mind immediately the question: Did I have a happy marriage? On some days yes, on some days no. I felt a faint resentment born of envy starting to throb. How dare she parade her marital success around for all to see? It was obnoxious. If I hadn't already read almost everything Patchett had written, the title might have kept me from reading further. But I had loved her novel *Bel Canto* so much that I was prepared to like anything Patchett wrote. With my newfound self-consciousness as a reader, I was looking for a counterpoise to Mankell; I wanted to see what I could learn from reacting to a world that sprang from an entirely different premise, and Patchett seemed ideal for the purpose. It was summer and I was living in the country, supported by my surroundings. In the mornings, when I walked down the driveway to see what the day was like, the presence of the mountains that faced me from across the reservoir provided massive reassurance. Whatever Patchett might say about marriage, I was game.

But I wasn't prepared for what I found. There's a wellspring of love in this book that resurges again and again and a level of verbal artistry that gave me a stronger impression of Patchett as a writer than I'd had before—as well as a severe case of envy. I didn't know which I envied more, her writing, or the love she had experienced.

I felt it first—that love—in an essay titled "The Wall," ostensibly about how Patchett took the entrance exams for the LAPD, but really about Patchett's love for her father, a retired policeman, whom her mother had divorced when Ann was four. When she describes how her father wrote all his telephone numbers down for each daughter on separate pieces of paper, with dates and times for calling, and Scotch-taped a dime to the paper next to each date, her love for him is not simply something she avers, it's something you feel the way you feel the sun on your face.

I warmed to the depth of her affection, which felt right and natural because it felt familiar: I had loved my own father without question or reservation, and when he died I did not feel separated from him. In my reaction to "The Wall" there was no envy. But "Love Sustained," the essay Patchett writes on caring for her grandmother, was a different story. It was the love that was the problem. Patchett took care of her grandmother in ways that were unappetizing and tedious: took her to the supermarket to buy groceries, dragged her to the department store to buy clothes, cut her toenails, washed her hair, brought her the fried fish fillets that were her favorite lunch. Having spent time with my aging mother over many years, I knew how hard it would have been to do all that for my mother with a good grace. The grace was the kicker. It made me think of how it had been between me and my mother. It wasn't what Patchett did for her grandmother that aroused my envy, but the spirit in which she acted. I felt the love motivating everything she did. Love underwrites every task and permeates the language. It was the love I envied. I had done for my mother as much or more than Patchett did for her grandmother, but I hadn't done it out of the same irresistible upwelling of affection.

Given that I lived far away from my mother and for most of those years worked full-time, I did what was possible for her after my father died. I visited her four or five times a year; every summer she came to stay with me and my husband for one or two weeks. As it became necessary, I consulted with doctors and social workers, hired caretakers and monitored her health, hired a bill-payer and found her a massage therapist, thought up things she'd like to do when I visited her in the retirement community where she lived, sleeping in the den on a foldout bed that poked into my back. I masterminded large parties for her seventy-fifth and ninetieth birthdays and when she turned ninety-five engineered a celebration in her birthplace, Manhattan. I bought clothes for her and things for her apartment, sent flowers and gifts and called her regularly on the phone. The phone calls were like rolling a heavy stone up a steep hill because my mother was hard of hearing and in the last years rarely had anything to say that wasn't a veiled, or an unveiled, complaint—with good reason, since she was lonely and, I thought, often depressed. I saw to it that she was visited by a nurse trained in psychotherapy for elders who called me after a year to say she didn't think my mother needed her. To me it was clear that what my mother needed was not professional help but friends—most of hers had died by then—friends, or a daughter nearby to keep her company. But my husband and I didn't want to quit our jobs and move halfway across the country to be near her. And, if she came to live with us, she'd have been cut off from the friends she did have, and from all the familiar people and places that made up the fabric of her life.

So instead, I did the things I've mentioned and many more, but there was often not much bounce or sparkle in the doing. It wasn't that I begrudged my mother anything, but that I felt a certain dryness in the execution, as if a fine dust had infiltrated the machinery as I went about my tasks. My good intentions sparkled when I arrived but fizzled as my attempts to cheer her went down to defeat. The dryness and the friction came not from anything I did or didn't do, but from my sense that nothing I did was ever enough. I felt I could never make up to my mother for her being alone, without her daughter nearby (I was an only child) and no grandchildren to be proud of. My mother had been a kindergarten teacher and loved children.

When I came to stay, what I felt from her, after an initial moment of being glad to see me, was an alternation between affection and disappointment, and underneath that, deep need and vaulting expectation, and beneath that, a kind of animal attachment that bound us together for life, as strong on my part as on hers. I wanted to please my mother and help her to be happy but rarely succeeded. Perhaps it was frustration with myself, disappointment in myself for not being able to satisfy her, that was the problem, not her and her situation. Being with her laid waste to my self-image. Besides failing to make her happy, and thus feeling powerless and incompetent, I was impatient at her deafness—having to repeat everything one says three times is a recipe for losing one's temper—and became irritated by her constant forgetfulness, conditions over which she had absolutely no control. At times, I turned into a short-tempered, brutal taskmaster, the very incarnation of a callous attendant. Being forced to see myself again and again in such an unattractive light shook me. I wanted not only to succeed in making *her* happy, I also wanted to be able to think well of myself.

Sometimes it comes to me that I will meet my mother in another life and there will be sympathy and mutual understanding between us; we'll be exhilarated, extravagantly happy, laughing, frolicking, raising our voices in perpetual celebration. In this life we'd both tried hard—she to be a good mother, I to be a good daughter—and on the physical plane we did well by one another, carrying out our responsibilities as fully as we could. Our disconnect was on the level of feeling. My mother's upbringing had been repressive; she never talked about what she felt—perhaps with her friends, but not with me. Though we each made a thousand overtures to one another, mostly they didn't take. I learned to try less often, and perhaps, so did she. Sometimes, when my mother was visiting with my husband and me in the country, at night she and I would go out to look at the stars together. My mother enjoyed seeing the constellations, many of whose names she knew and had taught me long ago. We would stand out in the driveway on the hillside, arms linked, staring up at the night sky, the spangled heavens in glory above us. While I like to remember those moments because they brought us close—I felt her soft hand and gentle breath, the warmth of her small body next to mine—in another way, we were as far apart as the stars themselves.

My mother's name was Lucy, speaking of stars, and when she was happy, light beamed from her Irish blue eyes. She liked to have fun. Her laugh was musical; in social situations she could get people to smile and laugh along with her; gaiety came to her naturally, and it was fun to be with her then. She loved playing games and was good at it, loved competing with other people at whatever the game might be. Sometimes this side of her made me anxious because, like my father, I was shy and noncombative and shrank from pushing other people out of the way. Despite the difference in our personalities we had good times together, when we shared a cigarette and a glass of sherry and a story about someone we both knew. Late in life, introvert that I am, I finally got it that my mother loved a party atmosphere. One Christmas when she was in her late nineties and parties were more or less behind her, I brought her a pair of teacups and saucers painted in green and red from a store in Chicago that sold gifts from Ireland. When I arrived, I gave her the present right away and made tea and found some cheese and crackers and cookies in the kitchen and we sat together on the old sofa that my parents had had since I was born and had a little party. For fifteen or twenty minutes it embodied the kind of good time my mother loved to have. In those moments we were happy. But still, our love was buried awfully deep, too deep to soften the rind that covered our hearts.

What I always wanted from my mother was to be seen and loved by her as I was, a person full of contradictory feelings—scared, impatient, idealistic, envious, enthusiastic, and brave despite my fears. I wanted her approval, not for the grades I got, or the plays I acted in, or the piano pieces I could perform—though I wanted her approval for these things, too—but for myself, raw and not yet ready for prime time. I wanted to be able to share my deepest fears and desires with her and not have to hold back. But although my mother encouraged me to strive for success, and not only appreciated my accomplishments but also helped me to attain them, she didn't want to know my doubts and fears. Weaknesses were not welcome. I understand now that my mother did not feel strong enough in herself to risk being implicated in another person's suffering or possible defeat, but while I was growing up and for many years afterward, I simply felt rejected.

As I've written all this down, certain things have become clear. I no longer mind but am glad that Ann was able to take care of her grandmother lovingly and without irritation, because I finally see that she is a different person from me and that her love for her grandmother doesn't mean that she is a better person. I had a different relationship with my mother from the one Ann had with her grandmother. There was the generational difference for one thing; grandparents and parents are not at all the same; we don't carry the same burdens in relation to the one as to the other. Ann wasn't an only child, she didn't have primary responsibility for her grandmother, and though I know nothing of her upbringing, on the evidence of her ability to feel and express love, I doubt her upbringing was the same as mine. The circumstances were different. The comparison didn't apply.

This realization sparked another: throughout this project, whenever I could, I put myself in the place of the people whose life stories I read, identifying with them as if they and I were one and the same person, adopting their points of view, sometimes criticizing them when they behaved badly, sometimes accusing myself of their faults, and comparing myself to them unfavorably when they exhibited admirable qualities I didn't possess. In short, I used reading not simply as an instrument of self-discovery but as a way to criticize myself. It wasn't that the discoveries I made were false; rather, I was too eager to point the finger of blame, too ready to see myself in a bad light and leave it at that. In exploring the parallel between Patchett's treatment of her grandmother and mine of my mother, I had gone over the ground carefully, paying attention to the circumstances, noting similarities and differences, and had seen that the cases were parallel only up to a point. There was no percentage in beating up on myself for not loving my mother as Ann had loved her grandmother, to do so would only make me feel bad for no good reason. It was time to put down the lash and stop flagellating myself, to stop turning insight into accusation.

Two months before she died, I came to live with my mother, sleeping in the den of her apartment—by that time, using my mother's credit card, I'd gone out and bought another sleep sofa that was less hard on my back. My mother was ninety-eight. In the last week or two, at night, after her caregiver had prepared her for sleep and turned out the light, I would come into her room to say good-night and hold her in my arms and talk a little and we'd be there together in the dark just the two of us, with the light from the living room coming in at my back, and it was then, shortly before the end that, one night, I felt the love that had always been there flow freely from her to me like water, slaking my lifelong thirst. It had always been there, this love, and it was heaven to feel it; it felt miraculous and at the same time completely natural. I can't imagine what it would have been like to have felt that love all along.

Thanks to Ann Patchett, I saw that I was not without love, but that in my case it flowed more easily from me to my father, whose love and approval I had rarely doubted, than it did from me to my mother, whose criticism I had felt throughout my life. I had done in relation to her the best I could, and, at the eleventh hour, I had felt my mother's love: it had been a glimpse of the promised land and I knew how lucky I was. I had gotten what I wanted, albeit for a very short time.

☽

But I wasn't finished with Patchett. Envy is not that easy to appease. There was still the question of her writing. Nobody, I grumbled to myself, should be allowed to write that well. Trying not to hold her virtuosity against her, I forced myself to reread the essay where Patchett describes how she had learned to write by doing nonfiction pieces for mass-circulation magazines. But that only made things worse. Not only was Patchett a wonderful writer, as demonstrated in this very piece, but she had had the perfect school to learn in. I was beside myself.

When she started out, Patchett thought waiting tables would be a good way to earn a living while working on her first novel and got a job waitressing at TGI Friday's in Nashville, where she was living with her mother. (Imagine envying that.) But the job turned out to be so exhausting that she had no energy left for her novel, so she tried the more traditional route of teaching creative writing. This didn't work out either. Supporting the creativity of others dampened her own creative urge, so she had to think again.

Patchett was no quitter; she was going to be a novelist no

matter what. She figured out that if she wrote nonfiction for the magazines she'd been submitting short stories to, she could earn enough money to scrape by while she worked on her novel. Making use of the connections she already had, and building on them, she set herself to learn how to give magazine editors what they wanted. The butcheries she had to perform on her prose in order to turn it into acceptable copy are hair-raising. But the hard, ego-battering work paid off. Patchett convinced me that working for the magazines was the only sort of training for a writer. Despite its grueling aspects, she made the work sound like fun. How I wished I had done that; it would have taught me so much about writing. Why hadn't *I* written for magazines instead of becoming a professor and writing for academic journals?

Well, I knew the answer to that. I never wanted to be a writer when I started out. I wanted to be a college professor. I went to an excellent graduate school, which was necessary for that kind of career, and, after a fifteen-year period of struggle, succeeded quite well. I had no reason to whine about not having had the right training for a profession I hadn't chosen. And I remembered why I hadn't chosen it: I didn't have anything to say. At that stage of my life I was still a blank slate. I had no cause to champion and nothing bad had ever happened to me. The only other career I'd considered—acting—I was afraid to pursue. The envy I felt was stupid—and greedy. I'd had a whole career teaching and writing literary criticism, work that I was passionately engaged with. It's just that Patchett's writing in this collection is so "sparkling," as the reviewer for the *New Yorker* put it, you can't help wishing you could write that way too.

Direct, down-to-earth, and well-crafted, the writing radiates confidence, draws us in, and makes us feel privy to the writer's inner thoughts. It also makes us comfortable. Her sentence rhythms set up expectations which she meets with answering rhythms. At all times we feel we're in the hands of an expert, we know each sentence will land on its feet, each point will be driven home. But there's more to it than that.

Every sentence has to do three things: grab the reader's attention, advance the line of thought, and have the right structure, tone, and rhythm. Miss out on any of these and you pay the price in loss of impact and momentum. The writing lesson distracted me from envy and focused me on the requisites of writing. Patchett taught me that, as a writer, what I needed was punch. I'd been trying to climb an ice mountain with worn-down sneakers and no gloves, slipping and sliding and not making a dent, while Patchett charged steadily upward wearing crampons, breaking through the ice with every step. She had punch.

Punch isn't just a formal feature of writing; it's also substantive. In Patchett's nonfiction the substance is personal experience, the great quivering chunks of it that her editors demanded and readers crave. In her magazine writing, Patchett digs deep, giving herself away piece by piece, using up her life in the service of her subject, whatever it happens to be. She's generous, offering up material central to her existence, like her marriage and her divorce—I, on the other hand, have always been afraid that if I write about what is most important in my life it will all be gone in no time and I'll have nothing left. Besides being generous with her experience, Patchett is also in touch with it, deeply; she knows what she feels and understands why she feels that way. In addition to generosity, there's wisdom and perceptiveness. And that's not all.

For writing to have punch, the author has to be 200 percent behind what she says. Conviction funds the enterprise. Once, in a sophomore course on modern literature in college, my professor, Miss Woodworth, told us she had written a novel which she gave to her sister to read. When her sister had finished it, she turned to Miss Woodworth and said: "Dorothy, you haven't the conviction of a wisp of thistledown." I was appalled. What a devastating and cruel remark. Its point, though, was unmistakable: without conviction, an entire novel can be weightless. Without conviction, you're nothing but a wisp of thistledown. So now I think that what I really envy in Patchett is how sure of herself she is. As long as I'm under the spell of her writing, I can feel sure of something, and it feels wonderful. How fortunate to know one's own mind that well. A line from Emily Dickinson keeps coming back to me: "On a columnar self / How ample to rely." I think Patchett must have a columnar self. Her essays have sequences in which the phrases and sentences succeed one another like the final chords of a symphony, crashing, triumphal, annihilating everything in their path. Their force is exhilarating. By the end, I'm bursting with their power. But as soon as I put the book down, the power is gone. It's her conviction, not mine.

And what do I know about Patchett, anyway? She was writing for mass-circulation magazines whose readers probably wanted to feel pumped up about something (who doesn't?), needed the adrenalin that her writing has in such large supply. She does say in passing that one of the things she had to learn was how to fake authority, so maybe she isn't as all-fired certain about things as she lets on. But no matter. I love the energy, I love the passionate conviction, and I love the command of her craft. Reading these pieces is like watching an Olympic gymnast perform, and, when I'm not feeling sorry for myself, the performance makes me feel tremendous. You go, girl, I want to say, right on.

Does Patchett have a columnar self? Is she as confident in her judgments as she appears to be? Maybe I'm attributing to her an assurance she doesn't have—at least not always. The mistake, in envy, is imagining that other people have it better and easier than you, that they have a secret, God-given ability that lets them succeed where you would fail. Thinking like this is hugely misguided, but I go on doing it. In the morning, I envy the young woman in running gear, loping easily along, enjoying the suppleness and strength of her body; in the afternoon I envy a writer I'm reading the subtlety of her psychological insights or the breadth of her research; in the evening I wish I looked like that movie star on TV. I'm an equal opportunity envier.

Whatever I'm envying at the moment—it can be anything from a haircut to a life of service to others—becomes the most important, most desirable thing in the world. Envy doesn't distinguish between trivialities and matters of ultimate significance. It's a posture, a stance toward life, a perpetual devaluing of self in favor of the (illusory) more gifted, more fortunate other. People imagine that life is easy for others, whose special abilities and optimal circumstances smooth their way. This is not true in any essential sense. Certain people have situational advantages or natural-born talents but nothing like what the envious person conceives. My father used to tell a story that makes this point.

Two men share a hospital room; one has the bed near the door, the other is next to the window. Every day the man with the view regales his roommate with accounts of what's going on out there—a romance, apparently, between a man and a woman who meet at a park bench. The man in the bed next to the door is spellbound. He thinks how great it would be if only he could have the bed next to the window. Then, one day, he gets his wish. The man next to the window takes a turn for the worse and dies. But when the other man is transferred to his bed and peers out to take in the view, he discovers that there's nothing there but a brick wall.

My father told this story more than once, and I loved listening to him tell it in his deep, storyteller's voice whose inflections were so full of kindness and promise. To my mind it was less about the selfishness and stupidity of the man next to the door than it was about the generosity and inventiveness of the man by the window, a man like my father, who loved to make up stories. For me, my father was the hero of the anecdote. It's not until now, remembering it, that I realize the story applied to me as well, the envious person in the bed near the door, and that this might have been why my father told it. But I also see that as a writer of nonfiction, I'm a storyteller, too. I don't invent things, it's not my talent, but I take my experience and make something of it, the way Ann Patchett does in these essays.

It never occurred to me to envy Patchett for having written *Bel Canto,* a novel that gave me so much pleasure I can remember not only where I was when I read it, on the deck behind our house in the Catskills, the sun declining behind the trees until it turned cool and I had to go inside, but also where I was when memories of the novel welled up in me again, as, driving home one day, I rounded the bends on the nameless stretch of road between the reservoir bridge and the turn-off for our house, and they flooded me with pleasure all over again. Memories of the love between the opera singer and the Japanese businessman, and of the love between the young revolutionary and the pianist. This novel is more full of love — romantic love — than any novel I have ever read. But what I'm saying now is that I never envied Patchett any of this, I simply basked in the experience, thrilled and amazed that someone could produce it just by writing. It was not *Bel Canto* but the nonfiction I was envious of — the wisdom, the passion, and the craft. But look, Jane, Ann lived the life that gave her that material; she earned the skill that gave her writing power. On that columnar self of hers be happy to rely.

☾

Time passes. I forget all about happy marriage — the subject of the title essay — can't even remember what it says. Happy marriage is a concept I no longer accept without question anyway; the idea irks me; I don't see it as a normal, taken-for-granted occurrence or condition, like a good meal or a sunny day. Marriage is simultaneously a minute-to-minute and a long-term thing — who can say what it is? When people say so-and-so has a happy marriage, who knows what they mean? And how do they know about someone else's marriage anyway? In her compendious report on male sexuality, Shere Hite observed that men are much more likely than women to say they're happily married, so there's a disparity of opinion at the most basic level—that of the individuals involved. You might think that having been in three different marriages and one serious relationship would have clarified things for me, but to the extent that it did, it was to show me that my aptitude for happiness in a long-term relationship was not outstanding and, more importantly, that my happiness in a relationship is more a function of who I am and how well I understand myself than of who the other person is. Not that that doesn't matter, but it need not be dispositive, as they say in the law.

In any case, I felt brave enough to circle back and reread Patchett's title essay, and what I found was that, although she believes her own present marriage is happy, she doesn't have a formula for how to have a happy marriage and doesn't believe there is one. And curiously, though the essay contains one spectacular scene that conveys the depth of love she and her husband have for each other, Patchett's account of her present marriage focuses mainly not on that relationship at all, but on her first marriage and divorce, a story full of suffering and bad decisions.

Patchett married, at a young age, a man with whom she was never happy and felt trapped in a relationship she didn't know how to get out of. Her account of how she struggled with guilt, almost dove into another doomed relationship, and finally broke free contains humor, irony, a shrewd grasp of her confusion and fears, and, throughout, a reassuring sense of self-acceptance. These qualities, which made her seem human, appealed to me more than the account of her present marriage, which was a bit too ideal. I didn't envy Patchett the admirable Dr. Karl, whom all his patients worshipped, and whom every woman in Nashville wanted to marry after his first wife left. It was the wry fact-facing, the combination of amusement and chagrin with which she recounts the history of her failed relationships that won me and made me want to be like her. Wanting to be like someone is not the same as envy: it's emulation, a less toxic state of mind.

When Patchett is tormented by the knowledge that she has to leave her first husband but can't bring herself to do it, a wise woman she calls Edra asks her a question. They're standing in a swimming pool:

> "Does he make you a better person?" Edra asked.... "Are you smarter, kinder, more generous, more compassionate, a better writer?" she said.... "Does he make you better?"
>
> "That's not the question," I said. "It's so much more complicated than that."

Patchett comments:

> [What Edra had said] was a piece of absolute truth, and while I rejected it as inapplicable to my very complicated twenty-five-year-old circumstances, I did not forget it. It worked its way into my brain and then stuck its foot in the door so that other bits of wisdom might follow, while back in present time I slipped beneath the surface of the water and swam away.

I love the way Patchett makes fun of herself as she rejects Edra's insight and slides deeper into the pool, seeing her own ignorance and forgiving herself for it. But Edra's question hooked me. *Does* my husband make me a better person, I wondered, smarter, kinder, more generous, more compassionate? I'd never thought of marriage like that. In no way does my husband resemble the wise, even-tempered, patient, altruistic Karl—in fact, a more opposite personality would be hard to conjure. My husband is smart, feisty, pragmatic, and fiercely loyal. Nor am I another Patchett. I was

failing this test. Identifying with the author 100 percent, as usual,
I came up short. But then I took two steps back and thought: is
the question—does he make you better—the right one to ask? If
self-improvement is the goal, don't give that job to your partner.
It's not up to him, or her. But, if I were to apply this standard to
my own marriage, I saw that though the dynamic between me and
my husband was different from that between Ann and Karl, the
result might not be all that different.

My husband, I realized, made me better by example. Some of
his many good habits had rubbed off on me—keeping my space
picked up, getting places on time, doing things when you think
of them and not putting them off, keeping social arrangements
simple—not to mention the pearls of wisdom he gave me when
it came to writing: have a steep angle of approach; transitions are
key. But the more important effect he had on me was bringing
out my worst side. The difference in our temperaments forced me
to look more deeply at myself. Had he not been aggressive and
combative, I never would have had to face my cowardice and self-
abandonment. Because he activated the patterns set down long
ago between me and my mother, I had to bring into consciousness and then examine all the ways I had bought into his version
of things without question, as I had with my mother, accepted
guilt and blame that weren't mine, took on roles he assigned to
me because I was afraid that if I objected I would be cast off, going along, unconsciously, to get along. His difference from me
forced me to see how I had avoided my fear of being left behind,
an outcast, and alone—a groundless fear, as it turned out. This
painful learning process is not over yet, but has it made me better?
Well, it's made me more of a grown-up, less likely to see myself as
a victim, more able to take responsibility for my situation. What
Patchett said was true: there is no one way for things to work.

Ann and Karl had been together for eleven years before they
got married, with Ann refusing because she couldn't stand the

idea of another divorce. Then one day out of the blue Karl goes to the Mayo Clinic for tests, one of which goes badly: it's his heart. When Ann learns of this, she insists on coming to Minnesota against his wishes. There's a blizzard in Rochester, the worst in ten years, and the chances of her making it are nil, the flight, horrendous. When Ann arrives, thirty seconds before Karl is wheeled into the operating room for a procedure, Karl, heavily sedated, turns to the nurse and says:

> "Didn't I tell you she'd be here?" He took my hand. "They said no, she can't make it. They said everything's closed. And I said you don't know Ann." And then he drifted off to sleep.
>
> Explain doubt to me, because at that moment I ceased to understand it. In return I will tell you everything I know about love.

The love Patchett feels for Karl surged through me as I read this. His total faith in her has extinguished all doubt, and her love for him moves into the stratosphere. It bursts from the page and fills me. After I came back to earth, my first thought was: I've never experienced anything like that. But slowly, over time, I came to a different realization.

When I think about Ann flying through a snowstorm to get to Karl, I see that our roles are reversed in relation to our husbands. In my marriage my husband is the one who comes through snowstorms; like Ann, nothing can stop him, and, like Ann, he doesn't mind. He doesn't mind going out of his way for me on a daily, even an hourly, basis and actually wants to do it. He doesn't mind picking up the things I've forgotten at the grocery store or taking my clothes to the cleaners. Cheerfully, he goes to the drugstore for my medication, takes my car in for an oil change, pays the insurance premiums, and keeps our tax records, keeps receipts for purchases, instructions for operating appliances, warranties, boxes that expensive items have come in, in case they have to be returned. He's the one who makes sure the air-conditioning filters get changed, sees to it that all our vacuum cleaners work, calls ahead and gets the TV and Internet service turned on when we move from one house to another. The other day, I had a flat tire and had to call AAA. When I saw that my card had expired, I didn't worry. I knew that my husband would have renewed my membership and that it wouldn't be a problem. He had; it wasn't. I'm ashamed to say that it has taken me a very long time to understand that these are the things that love is made of, that love isn't the words you want to hear at a certain time, or the perfect birthday present, or always being listened to and understood. Love is a person's constant outpouring of devotion in the language that he or she speaks and understands: in my husband's case, the language of action. It was embarrassing to admit that I had to read about the love in someone else's marriage before I could clearly see the love in my own. Not just to assume, or intuit, or infer it, but to see it in all its homely, palpable, and numberless manifestations. It's always been true of me that I didn't know how lucky I was, that I got caught up in envying other people when I was the one I should have been envying. How lucky to have discovered the extent of my husband's love before it was too late. How lucky is that?

On the way home from Rochester, Ann suggests that she and Karl marry right away, and they do. Mysteriously, Karl's heart, which according to the doctors had been irreversibly damaged, heals itself. A storybook ending if ever there was one. But if you think that in this chapter Patchett has reached her limit when it comes to writing about love, think again. After the chapter on marriage there's one on dogs that opens up a whole new dimension. It's called "Dog without End," but pursuing it would take me too far afield. I needed to take one last crack at Naipaul.

15

Self and Nature

Our house in upstate New York sits on the side of a hill in the western part of the Catskills overlooking the Pepacton Reservoir. It looks across to a range of wild mountains so lovely and reassuring that when I first saw them I thought to myself, "I could die here." The Pepacton, which is the dammed-up East Branch of the Delaware River, winds among the mountains for twenty-some miles and belongs to a system of reservoirs—the Cannonsville, the Neversink, the Ashokan, and the Schoharie—that supply New York City with water. The well water we drink in our house is cold and delicious.

When I first lived in the house I took long walks from it in all directions. Some instinct pushed me into the forest and kept me going for no definite reason. Sometimes the woods felt welcoming, sometimes hostile. Once, because the woods beyond looked so interesting, I wandered off into them from the old disused road I was on and got lost. It was early evening and the light was fading and I began to be afraid. I didn't know what to do. After a while our neighbor's dog started barking. By listening to where the barking came from I was able to orient myself, found my way back to the road before it got too dark to see, and got home all right. There was no harm done. But it had frightened me. I was not so in charge of things as I had thought.

There's a walk I used to take that circles the top of the hill we're on and comes out at the other end of our road. The walk always took exactly an hour and forty-five minutes and gave me a feeling of accomplishment—the hill was steep. I once took some new neighbors on this walk and the woman of the couple, who was younger than I, barely made it. Instead of regretting that I'd been thoughtless in taking her on this strenuous hike, I secretly felt proud that I was in better shape than she was. Now, because I can exercise hardly at all, I look on being in good physical shape, understood as a goal to be proud of, with some ambivalence, or even faint disdain. Nice work if you can get it. These days my walks are short and don't prove anything. I amble along, attracted by whatever the landscape has to offer, letting the forest clean me out. A walk in the woods is the best way to change your mood if you need to, as long as you don't let whatever's bothering you take up all the mental space. The thing is to relax, let your mind be unfocussed and let the forest do its work. Its work is subtle, ineffable, and beyond comprehension. Nothing you can put a finger on. I've found that even if I can't get a problem off my mind, being in the woods can still be effective. Stepping on leaves, earth, stones, and roots, looking at tree trunks, ferns, and rocks, stopping to look around, breathe the air and listen to the crows calling—something about this has transformative power. "Just as I am thou wilt receive, wilt welcome, pardon, cleanse, relieve," goes the old Gospel hymn, but its words, addressed to the Lamb of God, might as well be referring to the forest. Just as I am thou wilt receive. After you've wandered long enough in the woods, nature melts into your body, the forest becomes a balm and a refuge, a place that, if you submit yourself to it, will take care of you, not let you down.

Every day, over the ten-year period that he lived in a cottage on a Wiltshire estate, V. S. Naipaul went for a walk. The record he made of his observations and associated trains of thought in his novel *The Enigma of Arrival* shows that he underwent something like the mysterious rejuvenation and gradual rapprochement with nature I've been describing. *Enigma* is a quiet book, plangent and reflective, and, though it contains few facts about Naipaul's private life, highly personal. It had taken me a while, but I had finally come upon a work of Naipaul's that contained something of his essence.

The cottage from which he walks is the same cottage Theroux and his wife visited for one of the lunches described in *Sir Vidia's Shadow*—the cottage Naipaul and Theroux took a walk from that day, Naipaul naming all the trees and grasses, while the women did the washing up, the one outside of which Naipaul stood, whimpering in the dark, as Paul and Allison were leaving. Neither that visit nor any other Naipaul received while he lived in the cottage is mentioned in *Enigma*. Nor does he mention the fact that his wife, Patricia Hale, lived there with him the entire time. Naipaul's comings and goings, his routines (other than the daily perambulation), his social activities, the novels he's writing, his relationship with his wife are all off-limits. Yet one doesn't feel excluded. On the contrary, because he shares the daily walks and the ruminations they engendered, one feels taken into his confidence. The book is inwardly turned, and that inward turning is like an arm around the reader's shoulder: we, too, are going for a walk.

It's hard to exaggerate the extent to which *The Enigma of Arrival* differs from the novels that precede it. Never mind that it has few characters in the usual sense other than Naipaul himself, and no plot—nothing ever happens. Never mind that it's not really a novel but a memoir that calls itself a novel. The chief difference is in its emotional tone. A sense of loss so great that it can never be measured permeates the book. Its language is suffused with an elegiac feeling that rises to the surface at intervals and then retreats, but once felt can always be heard in the background. Meanwhile, the narrator walks, and the line of thought winds around, digresses, circles back on itself, and hovers, in a rambling, recursive movement that imitates the walk. The book feels fully grounded, more so than some of Naipaul's other work. For while it lacks the structural components of narrative—a plot, characters, events—it registers Naipaul's daily contact with a real place over a considerable period of time, and to the specificity of the setting it adds the emotional substance of Naipaul's inquiry into his past as a writer in exile. The recurrent pain of his recollections gives reality to what he's telling us, along with a pervasive sense that he accepts that reality and has come to terms with it, qualities notably missing in the two most famous books he wrote before *Enigma, In a Free State* and *A Bend in the River.* This contrast struck me again and again.

Those two novels, which, along with *A House for Mr. Biswas,* are generally regarded as Naipaul's most outstanding works of fiction, depend for their effect on our sense of the author's intellectual virtuosity. The narrative consciousness belongs to a person who stands aloof and criticizes everything that comes within his purview. They are chronicles of disappointment: the narrator's disappointment at the corruption and exploitation of colonial systems of power, and the venality, incompetence, and fraudulence of the postcolonial regimes that have taken their place. Naipaul's social critique reaches dazzling levels of sophistication, and, as in *A House for Mr. Biswas,* there are no images of nobility, compassion, or joy to relieve the sense of futility and waste. Nothing escapes the sharp edge of Naipaul's criticism, whether it's the oil on someone's collar, the discoloration of a wall, a vapid remark, or an act of deliberate cruelty. No matter where you look something is wrong: the official is dishonest, the waiter is sullen, the conversation is stupid, the hotel is dirty. Naipaul's readers play the role of collaborators in this project of finding fault, standing alongside the author, looking at first curiously and then disapprovingly down their noses, pleased to be credited, by association, with such a refined sensibility, such supple intelligence and worldly wise attitudes, for along with Naipaul, his readers now hold the key to understanding the world's deplorable condition. All in all, a heady experience, though in the end, a dispiriting one.

I disliked and was impressed by the brilliance of these novels in equal measure: despite their virtuosity, and to an extent because of it, they pushed me away, and so I left them alone. In varying degrees they repeated the distancing strategies of *Miguel Street* and *A House for Mr. Biswas*. In pondering my responses to those books I had already tried with limited success to achieve, in relation to Naipaul, a deeper level of sympathy and understanding. *The Enigma of Arrival* was different. In this novel, Naipaul gave me the feeling of companionship that I craved; rather than pushing me away, it let me feel close to him. Instead of sharply observed critique, there's contemplation, musing, and regret. Instead of being dominated by feelings of disappointment, disillusionment, and suppressed rage transmuted into cultural analysis, *Enigma* allows the reader to participate in an act of self-exploration, self-expression, and atonement. Naipaul, a stranger in a strange land, projects his loneliness onto the Wiltshire landscape and the landscape reflects it back. Conscious in the beginning of his alienation from the countryside he walks, he nevertheless records with meticulous tenderness the features before him, returning compulsively and fondly to certain objects and places, using the same words and phrases to describe them over and over in a rhythm full, simultaneously, of comfort and lamentation. The acts of description as well as the walks themselves soothe and relieve him. For the first time I found myself drawn to Naipaul as a person, rather than as a performer.

Every day he walks out from his cottage taking one of two paths, both of which lead eventually to a lookout point from which he can see Stonehenge. Every so often, he remembers a scene from his childhood in Trinidad which contrasts wildly with the countryside that surrounds him now, memories of sun and ocean that float mirage-like across the fields and downs. Though he's lived in England for many years, Naipaul feels himself to be an outsider, and as he traverses the landscape, making his way over roads and lanes, up hills and down dales, across grass and through puddles, day after day, covering the same ground again and again, gradually the land befriends him, and he it.

Change is the leitmotif that runs throughout his observations, change and decay. Though every day his walk brings him to a view of Stonehenge, he never approaches the monument itself but muses on the contrast between the megaliths standing on the plain and the highways surrounding them where cars and trucks whiz by, and between the ancient stones and the adjacent military installation where weapons are being tested. The past surrounded by the present. Closer to home there's the garden that Naipaul is drawn to and uses as a point of orientation and benchmark of change. Jack, a retired farmworker, grows vegetables, flowers, and fruit trees there, keeps ducks and geese, and tends the neat hedge that separates his land from the wide grassy droveway where Naipaul walks. Jack's place stands surrounded by disused farm buildings, discarded machinery, old tires, and other evidences of a life that has gone. The present surrounded by the past. He works steadily, shirtless in summer, making his corner of the world fruitful.

Then the farm on which Jack's cottage stands is bought by a conglomerate: a new storage shed goes up, a new sheep-shearing facility; large tractors appear. Cottages that had stood empty when Naipaul arrived are occupied by new workers, urban transplants whose lives are focused elsewhere, people who drive peppy little cars and don't fix their yards. Jack dies. His wife sells their furniture and moves away. The garden goes to seed. The ducks and geese disappear. The hedge, untended, doesn't last. Finally, one day, after being ill himself, Naipaul comes upon Jack's cottage and sees that it is being joined to the two abandoned cottages next to it to make a big, new house; the area where Jack's garden stood has been cemented over to form the forecourt. All these changes are registered in a quiet, almost impassive, way. But from time to time, Naipaul lets his feelings break through the surface details.

> The droveway, the way along the floor of the ancient river valley, was very wide. When I first went walking it was unfenced. In my first year, or the second, the wide way was narrowed. A barbed-wire fence was put up. It ran down the middle of the way, where the way was long and straight; and those sturdy green fence-posts (the thicker ones stoutly buttressed) and the taut lines of barbed wire made me feel, although the life of the valley was just beginning for me, that I was also in a way at the end of the thing I had come upon.

The slow pace, the repetition, the patient recording of detail, and, at the end, the feeling of loss—"although the life of the valley was just beginning for me, . . . I was also in a way at the end of the thing I had come upon"—all this is characteristic of the book as a whole. The mood is reflective, the affect both tender and sad, and beneath everything lies a calm, rueful acceptance of the way things are.

> How sad it was to lose that sense of width and space! It caused me pain. But already I had grown to live with the idea that things changed; already I lived with the idea of decay. (I had always lived with this idea. It was like my curse: the idea, which I had had even as a child in Trinidad, that I had come into a world past its peak.) Already I lived with the idea of death, the idea, impossible for a young person to possess, to hold in his heart, that one's time on earth, one's life, was a short thing. These ideas, of a world in decay, a world subject to constant change, and of the shortness of human life, made many things bearable.

The Naipaul who wrote this is not the man who casts aspersions everywhere. He freely admits his pain and without drama or fanfare invites the reader to become a witness to his suffering. He also invites us to take part in the process of healing that evolves as he walks every day down the wide grassy droveway, in sight of the water meadows and the downs, past the newly planted beeches and pines, past the ruined outbuildings, past Jack's garden and so around the turn to the right and up the incline to the lookout point. The repetitions that occur in his extended descriptions as he looks forward and backward, summarizes and analyzes, recalls and reflects, operate on us as they did on him, calming and steadying us with their rocking motion in the manner of a long tone poem or a lullaby, quieting and calming the spirit.

But make no mistake. Naipaul the critic is still alive and well. He does not pass up the opportunity to criticize the town fathers of Amesbury, the town he can see from his lookout, for putting up a sign with a coat of arms and a date: A.D. 979, and for causing Amesbury's churches and chapels and abbeys to be restored, calling attention to the historic nature of the place: "history, like an extension of religion, as an idea of one's own redemption and glory." This is the Naipaul we know: he interprets veneration for the past as an attempt to claim glory for oneself, disposing of both history and religion in a single gesture, dismissing them as self-deceiving modes of security seeking and self-aggrandizement. The judgment implies, of course, that Naipaul himself is above such stratagems and not in need of the comfort they provide. Still, he doesn't hesitate to add color to his own narrative by alluding to Guinevere's convent and the fall of nearby Camelot. He likes to recall the presence of Romans in the vicinity, and before them, the Druids. For him the point is not to associate himself with past glory, but to acknowledge the inescapability of death, which is what he thinks the people who go to restored churches are trying to avoid. He's at pains to differentiate them from Jack, who "on Sundays . . . worked in the morning in his garden, and went to the pub at noon, [and] in the afternoon . . . worked again in his garden." Naipaul approves of Jack, who is content with his square of earth and doesn't try to add anything to his stature by associating himself with past glory or future redemption. What Naipaul can't stand about the churchgoers and history worshippers is their attempt to do an end run around mortality. "Change and decay in all around I see," goes the old Protestant hymn, and Naipaul is in tune, but when it comes to the last line, "Oh, Thou who changeth not, abide with me," he's not.

When Naipaul scans the features of the countryside, his eye lights on the signs of transitoriness—trees that have been cut down, a new stand of pines recently matured, downs that have been cultivated for the first time, lanes that have been washed out, barns that have been renovated, houses that have fallen into disrepair. He focuses not just on change, but on decay; he is a poet of desuetude. When he goes to town he notices the shops that are failing; when he walks the grounds of the estate he notices the trees that have died under the weight of uncut ivy, the shrinking of the already shrunken vegetable garden, the way gates and doors formerly kept shut are allowed to gape open, and even to fall off their hinges and rot on the ground. Like Mankell, he's given to noting the unsatisfactoriness of things. And like Mankell he's unwilling to seek solace in anything beyond the material circumstances to whose deterioration he's been testifying. He struggles to accept change, he laments it, he bears witness to it.

Every time I picked up *Enigma* I became more convinced that it's Naipaul's masterpiece, especially as the topic shifted from the physical environment to alterations in Naipaul's worldview. He compares his present self to the boy who made the journey from Trinidad to London in 1950, flying to New York then shipping off to England. Naipaul looks back with compassion and regret on the eighteen-year-old who was embarrassed and ashamed because he let the airport taxi driver overcharge him, leaving him no money for tipping the hotel porter, the young man who ate a roast chicken brought from home over the wastepaper basket in his hotel room because his mother was afraid that there would be no wholesome food available on his journey, the young person who didn't realize he'd been given a berth on the ship in a better section than he'd been ticketed for, because he wasn't white and they had to stow him somewhere. He recognizes that these and other memories had been buried for years because they were too painful to recall and didn't furnish him with the kind of material he thought suitable for writing about. The pieces he'd written about the "Gala Night" aboard ship, and about Angela, who superintended the London boardinghouse where he'd lived, had neglected what was of real interest because he needed to make his subjects seem more cosmopolitan than they were and to come from a higher social class. The striving after cultural superiority and social distinction, rooted partly in his upbringing, was also a product of his colonial education, so abstract, so divorced from anything concrete that it led him to write articles on French cinema without ever having seen a French film. This education had created in him a fantasy England, the one he lost after he got off the ship, replaced by one that made him want to get back on.

The false assumptions he carried with him when he left Trinidad for England and the mistakes he made when he arrived are painful to recall and help to explain the book's title. It's taken from the title of a painting, *The Enigma of Arrival and the Afternoon,* by Giorgio de Chirico that Naipaul discovered in a book of reproductions he found in the cottage. The painting depicts the classical buildings of a port city, with a ship's mast and mainsail in the background. Naipaul invents a story about a man who arrives in the classical city, has a hard time there, and decides to return home, only to discover, when he arrives at the place where he had disembarked, that there's no longer any mast in the picture, no ship in which he can sail away. He has to stay in the foreign country.

Rehearsing this story, Naipaul realizes that it's his own. When he arrived in England from Trinidad he found it too strange, too lonely, too difficult to understand; England had forced him to see himself eventually as foreign and dark-skinned and impoverished, a cultural outsider, not belonging to an established social class. The dream he had had of England, in Trinidad, was shattered. But no matter how much he might wish to, he can't leave and go home. This is the enigma of arrival.

The sense of loss and feelings of sadness that arise again and again in *Enigma* made me feel I had something in common with Naipaul. Not that I felt like an outsider in places where I had lived or that I, too, was preoccupied with change and death: mine came from the losses my illness had brought me, and the isolation it imposed. The expression of sadness showed a softness of heart on Naipaul's part, a feeling of shared mortality so much more appealing than his sophisticated critiques of cultures and individuals. That he'd found a way to express his sadness rather than to bury or deny it I took as a sign of maturity. But I also came to realize, as I read further into the book, that it was not only sadness I had in common with him.

In the latter part of *Enigma,* which explains how Naipaul's view of the people he met on the estate altered over time, the tone darkens and the critical edge becomes more prominent. As I reflected on the return of Naipaul's faultfinding habit, I recognized it in myself, not for the first time. I had slowly been comprehending the power of negative habits of thought, mine as well as other people's, and had been appalled to realize, for example, that recently, on a thirty-minute car ride with my husband, every single thing that came out of my mouth had been a criticism or a complaint. The more I thought about it, the more I became aware that my criticism of Naipaul's faultfinding had a ludicrous side to it. I was coming to terms with the fact that I had an inner critic who was tirelessly at work, and that it was not only myself that I'd been criticizing ever since I could remember, it was everything. People and circumstances, clothing and furniture, books and movies, restaurants and hotels, food and wine, waiters and concierges, doormen and taxi drivers, tour guides and lecturers, stewardesses and salespeople—the list goes on forever because the criticisms arise, not from the objects themselves but from the viewer's state of mind. As I caught Naipaul in the act of identifying the precise manner in which some person he knew fell short, pointing out his vanity or gullibility or absence of resolve, I could no longer see myself as a blameless onlooker. In this regard the main difference between Naipaul and me was that his criticisms were shrewder.

A penchant for criticism and complaint does not come from nowhere: it is a consequence of pain—of blows received and of wounds sustained. Its point of view is that of an injured party, its set toward the world that of someone who feels assaulted or deprived of what they need. A sense of hurt and deprivation—conscious or not—increases the likelihood that one will find fault with one's environment, an inner darkness casting a shadow over the outer world and finding itself there. But in Naipaul's account of how his views of the people in the valley changed over time, although the scalpel is at work, in all cases except one the patient is allowed to live. The slowly acquired relationship with nature that had allowed embarrassing memories of his own past to arise and be forgiven has taken some of the unforgiving quality out of Naipaul's observations.

This is true of his portrait of Pitton, the last remaining gardener on the estate, a man who is not, as Naipaul had thought, a gardener by training, and who has no special relation to the soil, no traditional knowledge of the climate or of the local flora passed down from generation to generation. Pitton spends all his money on clothes in an effort to claim a higher social position than he actually has. Over time Naipaul's notion of him changes completely. And Pitton's idea of himself changes, too. When he's dismissed in favor of workers hired by the hour or the day, and his cottage must be sold for income, at first he's unable to take in the news. He stays on in his house, not looking for another place to live. Time passes. And then one day Naipaul sees Pitton driving a laundry truck and hears that he's been given an apartment on a council estate—a huge comedown for such a class-conscious person. But the new life suits him. He makes friends on the council estate, forgets about drinking champagne with his old employer, and in the end no longer even acknowledges the author when they pass on the street in Salisbury.

Like Pitton, Naipaul has let go of attitudes that had formed his earlier self. Though it's not his natural inclination, Naipaul is teaching himself to embrace change and recognizes that this dismantling of old assumptions has become his subject. The book is a beginning again, a reseeing of himself actuated by a reseeing of his past. To illustrate the way in which he comes to change his mind about Pitton, he writes that one day close to Christmas he took Pitton a bottle of whisky as a present. Pitton was a long time coming to the door—presumably because he was making himself presentable—and Naipaul has time to look around. The gardener accepts the gift with no enthusiasm, and Naipaul realizes he's made a mistake. Pitton doesn't want him there because he's made no improvements in the cottage, which he has occupied for a long time: the furnishings are drab and the building is in a state of disrepair. Naipaul interprets these facts as the key to who Pitton really is: not the well-heeled, self-sufficient person he presents himself as—and who Naipaul had believed him to be—with an outfit for every occasion, but a dependent who doesn't fix up his house because it doesn't belong to him, and invests his money in clothing to be worn outside his house, pretending to have more money than he does, a man who feigns independence but is in fact servile.

Putting up a good front is something Naipaul understands—he remembers how the people he grew up with did it in the presence of persons who outranked them socially—and he himself, as one learns from *Sir Vidia's Shadow,* has the same tendency, dressing always in English tweeds, carrying a walking stick, becoming a wine connoisseur, and keeping an apartment in London at a good address. According to Theroux, Naipaul claims to disdain most of the people he meets, but it's obvious that he cares deeply what other people think of him and is sensitive to situations where power and status are involved: he knows why Pitton didn't want him to see the way he lived. If he were in Pitton's place, Naipaul would not have wanted him to see his house either.

The understanding Naipaul extends to Pitton is dry and unsentimental but not to be underestimated. His ability to penetrate another person's façade can seem pitiless, even cruel—his description of the window of a dress shop in Salisbury that has fallen on hard times as testimony to its proprietor's loss of heart and failure of will is a stunning example. The precise analysis is not the result of mercilessness but of comprehension: when Naipaul describes the owner's discouragement, her desire to give up altogether and hide from the world, it's the harshness of his own experience that he's expressing. His ability to identify other people's discouragements and failures comes from having been able, on his extended perambulations throughout the valley, to see the pathos of his own history as a naïve outlander, a somewhat misguided transplant who struggled for a long time to find his bearings and to feel at home. Now that finally, after all these years, he has begun to take root and feel himself welcomed by the landscape where he lives, that sense of being accepted allows him to extend acceptance to others and also, possibly, to himself.

Here, though, as in his other work, Naipaul's attention focuses primarily on other people: though sadness permeates the language of *Enigma,* the habit of observing others and describing them coolly from a distance persists. There's one passage which reveals how much sympathy he can have for another person when he recognizes, consciously, the parallels that exist between his experience and theirs.

One day, after he's left the estate and moved into the cottage he'd had renovated nearby—actually two shepherd's cottages made into one—a car comes down the lane. An old woman gets out and peeps through the hedge. She's not sure she's come to the right place. As a child, she'd spent summers in one of the cottages with her grandfather; she remembers the lane, how it narrowed to a footpath, and then to a footbridge over the river where she used to go to a farm every day for milk. But the cottage is no longer there. Naipaul:

> I was horribly embarrassed. Embarrassed to have done what I had done with the cottages, all the things that had disorientated the old lady and made her question where she was. . . .
>
> . . . I was also embarrassed to be what I was, an intruder, not from another village or county, but from another hemisphere; embarrassed to have destroyed or spoilt the past for the old lady, as the past had been destroyed for me in other places, in my old island, and even here, in the valley of my second life, in my cottage in the manor grounds, where bit by bit the place that had thrilled and welcomed and reawakened me had changed and changed, until the time had come for me to leave.

After all the withering comments that Naipaul has made about other people in his writing, his making common cause with the old lady is an occasion for wonder. This time he doesn't dwell on a faulty surface detail; he actually imagines the old woman's inner life—her desire to relive the past, her confusion at the disappearance of her grandfather's place. He identifies with her—they've both lost a part of their childhood—and is horrified that he himself has been the cause of such a loss for another person. Once again the plangent tone revives as he speaks not only of his lost childhood but of the loss of the valley as it was when he first came there—the insistent need to rehearse the feelings of deprivation signaling how deep they run. In passages like this, where the attitude of contempt is put aside, and the pain that caused it is allowed to surface, I can't help feeling that the real Naipaul has emerged at last.

Naipaul speaks of his time in Wiltshire as a reawakening, a second birth, a healing. Though he did a great deal of traveling while he lived there, the cottage on the estate and the surrounding countryside served him as a refuge, a place that recognized him when he returned to it, a source of solace and renewal. Naipaul's grateful acknowledgment of that beneficent relation made him seem more human to me. I had felt the same gratitude for the chance to walk abroad in the mountains whenever I wanted, and for the effect the landscape had on my psyche and spirit. I began to wonder how walking those paths over the years might have changed me. I couldn't claim a second birth or a reawakening but rather a nameless feeling that my being was part of the mountains and the reservoir I'd been in the presence of for so long, a sense that I had something in common with the trees and the ferns where I walked and that who I was was connected to what they were. Shortly after I finished rereading *Enigma,* I came across a piece of writing that illuminated this relation for me, and shed light on the transformation Naipaul had undergone as well.

The book group I belong to in the Catskills decided to read *The Man Who Mistook His Wife for a Hat and Other Clinical Tales* by the great neurologist Oliver Sacks, who had recently died. In the book, Sacks discusses the case of a man he names William Thompson, whose amnesia was so severe that, from moment to moment, he could not remember where he was, who he was with, or who he himself might be. In conversation, to fill in the gaps, he created numerous identities for himself and his interlocutors, passing from one invention to the next with marvelous energy and imagination in a ceaseless stream of confabulation which seemed ultimately meaningless, for his disability made it impossible for him to *be* a specific person. Here is Sacks's description of how William Thompson was sometimes able to retrieve a coherent sense of self. The final paragraph in a chapter titled "A Matter of Identity," it struck me as applying to my own experience and to the change that befell Naipaul as he walked the grounds of the Wiltshire estate and the countryside beyond:

> Our efforts to "re-connect" William all fail—even increase his confabulatory pressure. But when we abdicate our efforts, and let him be, he sometimes wanders out into the quiet and undemanding garden which surrounds the Home, and there, in its quietness, he recovers his own quiet. The presence of others, other people, excite and rattle him, force him into an endless, frenzied, social chatter, a veritable delirium of identity-making-and-seeking; the presence of plants, a quiet garden, the non-human order, making no social or human demands upon him, allow this identity-delirium to relax, to subside; and by their quiet, non-human self-sufficiency and completeness allow him a rare quietness and self-sufficiency of his own, by offering (beneath, or beyond, all merely human identities and relations) a deep wordless communion with Nature itself, and with this the restored sense of being in the world, being real.

Naipaul didn't suffer from amnesia, but he did have a problem of identity: a person of Indian descent, raised in relative poverty as a Hindu, on an island with a majority African population under the authority of a British colonial regime, he travels to the seat of colonial power, there to win for himself the highest possible distinction as a man of letters—he is soon to be knighted and will eventually win the Nobel Prize—and finds himself living deep in the countryside of this alien land where, mysteriously, his feelings of unease and placelessness begin to abate. His malady and William Thompson's are not so different as they might seem; in both cases the cure is the same. A deep wordless communion with nature helped Naipaul to heal from the nightmares of his existence and find at least for a while a sense of peace and self-sufficiency that had heretofore escaped him; walking to within sight of Stonehenge every day, he achieved what Sacks describes as "the restored sense of being in the world, being real." No wonder he called his time in the valley a second birth. Sacks's eloquent account of how nature affects one's sense of identity transformed my idea of what identity might mean. It corresponded to the experience of an expanded self which I felt gazing at the mountains and the reservoir and walking the forest paths. Naipaul's walks in the valley, his experience of belonging to the peace of a nonhuman order, existing apart from any human or social demands, had made his rebirth possible. That is why *The Enigma of Arrival* has no plot, no characters, and no events: there is no human drama here as we are accustomed to know it. Rather it is the tracing of an evolution, the patient, meticulous record of how a person, freed from the demands of society and from its rewards as well—think of those literary prizes—can find himself or herself "beneath, or beyond, all merely human identities and relations."

16

The World Is What It Is

Naipaul published *The Enigma of Arrival* in 1987. In 2008, Patrick French published, to wide acclaim, *The World Is What It Is,* an authorized biography of Naipaul that won the National Book Critics Circle Award. It's a stunning book by any measure—a wealth of information masterfully handled, disturbing facts interpreted with cool intelligence. But the main impact comes from the shock of learning what kind of life Naipaul actually led. Anyone who had read *The Enigma of Arrival* would soon realize that the picture Naipaul drew of his life when he lived in the cottage on the Wiltshire estate bore only a partial resemblance to reality. Though the picture he drew was true as far as it went, it didn't begin to convey the chaos and misery of Naipaul's life at that time.

When I read the biography it was a devastating experience. Not just because I'd known so little about Naipaul's life—the truth was like a body blow—but because I identified with his wife, Pat, whose suffering and humiliation were, according to French, beyond anything I could have imagined. So much so that setting out to write this chapter, I feel shaky and afraid of what I'll have to face about myself, afraid of saying things I'll regret, afraid of skewing this book too much in the direction of pain— Naipaul's, Pat's, my own. But there's no getting around it.

The awfulness of Naipaul's treatment of Pat is at the center of French's book. The story starts innocently enough: in 1950 Vidia and Pat were first-year students at Oxford, both were outsiders in the university environment—she a woman, he an East Indian from the West Indies—both from poor families, both talented and deeply insecure. She was nice-looking and intelligent; he was gifted and magnetic. They had a common interest in literature: he wanted to be a successful writer, and she liked the idea of furthering his career. Though even at the beginning she provided more support to him and his work than he returned to her, it was a way of living that seemed to suit them; they were one another's refuge. The cracks in their relationship appeared almost immediately.

Pat was acting in college theatrical productions and Vidia objected to her appearing before an audience in makeup and gaudy clothes. Though she argued in the letters she wrote him, cogently and succinctly, that their partnership should not mean the end of her ambitions, he couldn't tolerate the notion of her exposure on the stage—said it went against his Hindu upbringing. He objected so strongly that she stopped acting. And that, in effect, was that: the end of Pat's chance to be a player, not just on the theatrical stage but on any stage at all, the end of her chance to have an independent existence. Vidia's work and Vidia's needs dictated the shape of their lives from then on. In place of a career, Pat took pick-up teaching jobs that would accommodate Vidia's schedule and provide them with financial support. Though she tried to write when Vidia was off doing journalistic research— she was a good writer and over the years published three or four substantive articles in British periodicals—she had trouble bringing the pieces she started to closure. Weakened by her subservient relationship to Vidia, she lacked the confidence and the drive to persist. If she had had children, it might have made her life more fulfilling, but they were not able to have children together, which increased her sense of isolation and feelings of impotence.

Her subordination to Naipaul undermined severely her efforts to have her own life. Pat could not assert herself effectively in the relationship and sabotaged herself by assuming all the blame when things went wrong. Judging from her diaries and from French's comments, Pat had almost no feeling of self-worth and would not risk putting herself forward either socially or professionally. She used her acute literary intelligence as the first critic of Naipaul's writing—he trusted and relied on her judgment—and derived satisfaction from the thought that he valued her opinion as much as that of Francis Wyndham, editor and writer, one of his early supporters. It was on her devotion and service to Vidia that what self-esteem she had rested.

As a couple Pat and Vidia were unhappy, sometimes desperately so. Vidia had little sexual interest in Pat. After a while they slept in separate rooms and seemed to have had sex only at long intervals, though from time to time, according to French, their sex life would revive. Early in their married life, Vidia started visiting prostitutes on a regular basis, a practice that went on for many years. A few years before Pat died, Naipaul gave an interview to the *New Yorker* in which he talked about having been "a great prostitute man." It made headlines in the international press, and that is how Pat found out. It nearly destroyed her. In fact, it may well have. In an interview with French after her death, Vidia admitted that Pat's breast cancer, which had been in remission for a few years, recurred shortly after she got this news. She died not long after.

Comparatively speaking, though, Naipaul's practice of having sex with prostitutes was the least of Pat's worries in that regard. In 1972, on a visit to Argentina to do research for an article commissioned by the *New York Review of Books,* Vidia met Margaret Gooding, an attractive young Anglo-Argentinian. Though she was married and had three children, Margaret had already had a number of lovers and, according to French, was bored with her life. Naipaul wanted her the minute she walked into the room. But he had no sexual self-confidence and didn't know how to court a woman. He relied on a mutual friend, Norman Thomas di Giovanni, to make arrangements that would give him a chance to win her over, which he finally managed to do. To say that their affair was tempestuous would be an understatement. Despite frequent explosions, verbal and physical, Vidia and Margaret were passionately attracted to and obsessed with one another. The sexual relationship was one of domination and submission—an arrangement they both enjoyed, involving physical violence on both sides, and, on Vidia's side at least, beating. (He beat her.)

At first, it was wonderful; Vidia felt reborn. There's a picture of him in the biography, taken by Margaret, in which his body language has completely changed: he stands there, one foot on a low wall, wearing a polo shirt, looking relaxed, self-confident, and happy. Vidia's work went into high gear: his prose became suppler, energized, his novels more inventive, their impact more powerful. He freely acknowledged that his relationship with Margaret had given his work new energy. It was after he met Margaret that he wrote *A Bend in the River,* which is often considered his best novel. He was living in the Wiltshire cottage at the time, carrying on with Margaret while doing research abroad, but always coming home to Pat. Outwardly and inwardly he veered back and forth between the two women, at one moment deciding to be faithful to Pat and telling Margaret good-bye (he would call his friends and tell them that he was doing this), only to change his mind and declare to Margaret that they would be together soon, for good. This happened again and again.

In light of these things, one might ask, what is the truth of Naipaul's claims in *The Enigma of Arrival* to have been resurrected by his walks in the Wiltshire countryside? Was he not healed? Did he not undergo a second birth? Although on the surface the facts seem to contradict Naipaul's claims, I don't think they invalidate his account. When he lived in the cottage Naipaul's life was in turmoil. Careening back and forth between Margaret and Pat, unable to choose between them, he must have needed and welcomed to an unimaginable degree the impersonal presence of the trees and the water meadows, the droveway and Jack's garden and the view of Stonehenge. Nature provided him with a third space, a peaceful, nonjudgmental environment to which the tortured state of his allegiances was completely irrelevant. His work afforded him another kind of haven. Between the two, he was able to survive.

In the second year of the affair, Naipaul told Pat about Margaret. Shocked and humiliated, she left the cottage and went to stay at their London flat, but not before comforting and soothing Vidia, who had presented the information in a grief-stricken manner. Not long after, she returned to Wiltshire to resume her wifely duties. Naipaul's friends urged him to stay with Pat, at first because they felt it was unfair of him to abandon her, and later because they doubted Pat was strong enough to manage on her own.

The facts are painful enough by themselves. But their tragic consequences can only be felt by reading Pat's journals, which French quotes from copiously. They are full of incidents in which she agonizes over his mistreatment of her, for, in addition to carrying on his flagrant affair with Margaret while abroad—everyone knew—Naipaul went into sudden rages at home, shouting at Pat, calling her names, and behaving like an ungovernable child, all of which sits side by side with Pat's account of catering to his needs, making meals for his guests, carrying pillows into his bedroom, and taking dictation in the middle of the night.

Here's an example. After Vidia told Pat he was going to move into Dairy Cottage by himself—Dairy Cottage was the name given to the two cottages he'd had renovated when they had to leave the cottage on the estate—she wrote in her diary:

> I went on forlornly, going on about being treated as an equal.... He looked for a clean vest, I produced his present favorite sleeveless style from the airing cupboard and looked out, at his request, another

thermal top, asking whether he has a washing machine in Dairy Cottage. Yes it's all waiting there ready. My stomach turned over.

Not long after, Vidia changed his mind about their living arrangements. He and Pat lived in Dairy Cottage as man and wife, though they spent much time apart, one in London, the other in the country.

As Vidia's reputation grew, so did his anger at the slightest unpleasantness; his statements in interviews became more outrageous, his domestic behavior more impulsive and damaging. Pat writes:

> Simply these days, I regret the loss, the damage, of Vidia's rages and quarrels. Simple losses—of the beautiful food I have cooked, happy days, days of one's life. It was my fault: I was anxious and told him not to "overdo" it when he proposed to go out. . . . [What follows is her recounting of what had happened]. He was resting, the weather, sunshine & breeze, so lovely and I was wishing he would come out. He cheered up; he was whistling. He dressed in his old khaki cotton trousers and the green polo checked cotton sweater and straw hat. At my words [telling him not to overdo] he struck his head and burst out, "the bitch" etc and went back up, removed the clothes & put indoor clothes on, heavy dressing gown & switched on the heat in his bedroom. "Don't speak to me" etc. "I shall only despise you more."

Pat's account is made more painful because she blames Vidia's behavior on herself. It's as if she were afraid that someone might blame her for what happened, and she rushes to criticize herself before anyone else could. Or perhaps she doesn't trust herself to see the situation as it is—Vidia is abusing her, and she is putting up with it. Probably both. At the same time, one can feel Pat's affection for Vidia in the detailed way she describes his old khaki cotton trousers and the green polo checked cotton sweater—and through that feel the bind she was in. She had loved this man and had given up her life for him—her identity and sense of self-worth were bound up with his career—how could she back away from all that? But she was desperately unhappy; after learning about Margaret, she spent years not knowing what to do with herself, how to be, whether to stay or to go. After a while, as one reads deeper into the book, it is Pat, the self-effacing and subservient, the weak, ineffectual, unaccomplished member of the couple, who takes over the biography, providing it with depth and dimension. Without the basso continuo of Pat's self-sacrifice, the story of Naipaul's life would not be nearly so compelling.

I identified with Pat and felt her suffering keenly, but Margaret's plight was equally terrible. Her relationship to Vidia was incandescent in its intensity. When asked by a reporter to describe his vision of earthly bliss, it was Margaret Vidia was thinking of when he replied: "the delirium of reciprocated passion." Nevertheless, Vidia did not treat Margaret any better than he treated Pat. Aside from physically beating her, Vidia betrayed her trust. After being assured by him many times that they would be together, Margaret took the decisive step of leaving her husband, which meant giving up her children as well. Living alone, missing her children, her relationship with her parents strained, and, in order to support herself, doing jobs that French describes as "soul-destroying," she pined for Vidia, who remained in England and who, not long after she had implemented her decision, recanted his. Phoning her in Argentina, a month after he had promised her they would be together soon, he said: "Feel yourself free." Margaret was incredulous and distraught. But the relationship continued as before, with Vidia taking her along with him on research expeditions, or stopping to see her on his way home, only now Margaret was alone in Argentina and had to work at whatever she could get in order to live.

Three times over the years she became pregnant with Naipaul's child. When informed of the pregnancies by mail, Naipaul did not write back. Three times, she had an abortion. After the third, she remarked to Vidia in a letter that it was as if these matters were too unimportant for him to notice. For twenty-four years Naipaul carried on in this way, with violent eruptions in the relationship from time to time, taking Margaret with him while he traveled, sometimes seeing her in London when she visited her sister, always in the end coming back to Pat. Things did not end well.

Shortly before Pat died, Vidia had been traveling with Margaret in Indonesia. He was full of guilt. Pat was in the hospital. He had sent a loving fax, asking what he could do for her, and she replied, keep on with your work, his question had been enough. French continues: "In his head, Vidia began to reject the mistress who had through decades of harassment chosen to stand by him. . . . Now that he might, if things went badly, have Margaret as his wife, he had a fateful, hateful, fatal sense that he did not want her in his life any more." In an interview with French some years later, Naipaul said: "I feel that in all of this Margaret was badly treated. I feel this very much. But you know there is nothing I can do. . . . I stayed with Margaret until she became middle-aged, almost an old lady."

Besides Margaret's age, there was another reason Naipaul didn't marry her. After being in Indonesia—he was working on a book on Islam—he went on to Iran and Pakistan; Margaret did not like Pakistanis and had gone home. While he was in Lahore, Vidia met a journalist named Nadira Khannum Alvi. After two weeks he asked her to marry him. When Pat, who was by that time dying, called his hotel, Nadira answered and passed her on to Vidia. Pat asked, "Was that Margaret?" Naipaul replied, "No, no, that was someone else." As if this were not enough, instead of returning to England, Naipaul continued on to Malaysia, "anxious," as French puts it, "that neither the prospect of looming death nor marriage should interfere with his work." Though at some time during this period Vidia let Pat know that he had met a lover in Pakistan (Pat remarked to a friend that it would be easier for them when she was gone), he didn't tell her that they planned to marry; nor could he bring himself to inform Margaret. He was no longer communicating with her. She learned about the marriage from the newspapers.

The treatment Naipaul meted out to his first wife and his mistress extended to his friends as well. I've discussed how things ended between Vidia and Paul Theroux. The brutal severing of a thirty-year friendship on a London street was followed up by a comment he made about Theroux's work: "He wrote tourist books for the lower classes." Of Anthony Powell, author of the twelve-volume *Dance to the Music of Time,* with whom he'd been friends for many years, he remarked: "It may be that the friendship lasted all this time because I had not examined his work." In a news interview Naipaul once said: "I have no friends," giving as his reason "the twists and turns of a long creative career," though it would seem that it wasn't so much that he never had any friends as that he dropped them when they became inconvenient.

It's impossible not to be repelled by the way Naipaul behaved toward the people he knew—intimately or otherwise. When I tell people about his life, usually their reaction is to say, in so many words, what an asshole! They dismiss him out of hand. Everyone feels sorry for Pat and Margaret. As told by French, the story of Naipaul's life inevitably provokes this response. But there is more to be said. As I've mentioned, reading the biography the first time, I was upset for days. The second time through wasn't much better. Not just because of the facts but because of my identification with Pat. Seeing myself as a version of her nauseated me and threw me off balance: is this who I really am, at heart? I asked myself, horrified. Is this how I'm seen by other people? As handmaiden to an important husband? The identification, though, allowed me to go beyond the picture French paints into the dynamics of Pat's relation to Vidia. There's another side to her story—and to Vidia's as well—at least one other—and it needs to be heard.

Having been in a marriage where I allowed myself, for years, to be shouted at, blamed for minor disruptions of the domestic order—forgetting to call a repairman, leaving a wet glass on the kitchen counter—and furiously attacked for things I did that I thought were innocent—the one I remember most clearly is getting an estimate for the cost of renovating a kitchen sustainably—I know what it's like to be in Pat's shoes. Though my marriage is not like hers in most other respects, in this one there was some similarity. From time to time, when the pressure mounted, I would suggest to my husband that we see a couples therapist: we would go for a while, the explosive behavior would go underground and things would seem to be all right, until it happened again. Sometimes, I would just go off by myself and think through what it would be like to leave and realize that I could do it if I felt I had to. This gave me a sense of independence and strength that allowed me to feel better in the relationship. But I did not recognize how damaging the situation had become until one day someone told me outright that she couldn't stand the way my husband treated me. It saved my life. I saw then the position I had allowed myself to be in—the psychological punching bag position, let's call it—and knew I couldn't take it for one minute more.

The therapy that ensued this time made an enormous difference. My husband's outbursts dwindled to nothing. As for me, I had to confront the fact that I had allowed the verbal attacks to go on all these years and therefore bore some responsibility for them. I realized that the reason I'd done so lay in my upbringing. I had been trained by my mother to occupy the position I was in in my marriage—it fit like a glove—because it was exactly the one I'd been in in relation to her. I'd caved in to my mother early on. She had me under her thumb. I never talked back to her or contravened her wishes. There was no adolescent rebellion. No flouting the rules. As a therapist pointed out to me, parents don't teach their children to defend themselves, because what they want is obedience. I obeyed. I toed the line and strove for approval; at home and in school I became a performer and an achiever. I lived up to the wishes and expectations of people in authority, not because I was forced to, but because I wanted to. I didn't know anything else.

In my professional life, by contrast, I became a rebel and a game-changer. In my scholarly work I took controversial positions that exposed me to attack and ridicule, something which I both feared and enjoyed. As a teacher, I experimented wildly. Thinking of myself as courageous—I saw my husband as courageous, too, it was one of the main things that had attracted me to him—I tended to be impatient with people who struck me as cautious and self-protective. To my timidity in close relationships I was blind. For the truth was, when there was friction or turmoil at home or with friends, I avoided confrontation and smoothed things over, retreated into myself, and hoped that it all would pass.

The couples therapy showed me that it had always been in my power to stand up to my husband and that I hadn't done it because I simply was not equipped. I'd had no brothers and sisters at home to defend myself against, and no experience challenging the authority of my parents, especially my mother. I didn't know that going up against a person I was close to need not break the relationship for good because I had never tried. Accommodation was what I was used to. As far as I knew, it was that or nothing. I'd been married twice before; failing at marriage a third time was unthinkable. So I accommodated.

The point I'm making is: outrageous as Naipaul's behavior toward Pat was, she could have spoken up. She could have drawn the line early on when he insisted she stop acting in plays. Her letters indicate that she saw the unfairness of the relationship, but she did nothing about it. Her subservience was a choice. If worse came to worst, she could have left him. It certainly crossed her mind. French says that, in the final years of their marriage, Pat told her sister at lunch one day that she was going to separate from Vidia. What I'm getting at is that the easiest and most natural way to read the biography—with Naipaul as villain and Pat and Margaret as victims—is not entirely fair or accurate. Both women chose to occupy the roles they played. French supplies ample grounds for such a reading and points the reader in that direction more than once. Of course, the Bluebeard version (monster vs. martyrs) is easier and more satisfying to adopt, in that it puts one on the moral high ground, and is freer of complications and ambiguities. But it does not take everything into account. In fact, it robs both Pat and Margaret of the dignity of being choosers of their own destiny—however tragic or painful that destiny was.

One can argue that for Pat to have left Vidia at the beginning of their marriage would have been extremely difficult. It was England in the late fifties, early sixties; the British are more sexist, as a culture, than Americans are, and women's liberation had not yet become a force. Pat would have had to make her living teaching in secondary schools; she would have had to live frugally, and, though she seems to have been well-liked by the people she and Vidia socialized with, being an introvert, she might have had trouble finding friends. Her parents would no doubt have been scandalized. Her prospects were drab and lonely. By the nineties, when Pat told her sister she was going to separate from Naipaul, social opinion on divorce had changed dramatically. For most of her married life, it would have been very hard for Pat to leave Vidia, but not impossible. It would have taken enormous strength of purpose and clarity of vision. As a reader of Naipaul's work, it seems that Pat possessed these qualities in abundance. But there appears to have been nothing in Pat's background and education that helped her to develop the courage and perceptiveness she needed to act in her own behalf in a close relationship. In that sense, we were similar. Still, the option was there.

Whenever I think of the relationship between Pat and Vidia, I cringe at the resemblances between Pat and myself. She makes me scrutinize my own behavior, question it, shake my head at my self-ignorance and fearfulness. Her story forces me to criticize the way I was brought up, shows how sometimes the Christian values of love and forgiveness can destroy the person who attempts to practice them, can erode their self-esteem, cover up their weakness and their fear, and enable others to be neglectful and even abusive toward them. Her example has impressed on me the necessity for women, in particular, when they're growing up—destined as so many of us are to fulfill the role of caretakers and pleasers—to be encouraged to develop firm boundaries, to have confidence in their own judgments and instincts, to value their own needs and wants as much as other people's. Above all, it illustrates how the desire to be good and unselfish can be the ultimate in self-subversion and self-betrayal. But despite all this—and I have spent hours analyzing the resemblances and differences between me and Pat, weighing the pros and cons of her behavior—the spectacle of Pat's life brings me to a point where I no longer find it appropriate to question her values, her choices, her actions or her inaction. Finally her story leaves me mute, not wanting to point a finger anywhere, not wanting to judge.

I would rather let Patrick French's biography stand as a reminder of, and a monument to, Pat's meekness and her pain; there is heroism in her self-sacrifice as well as ignorance and confusion. I would rather let the record of my encounter with her be an act of respect and commemoration. There is a better way to honor her than through self-analysis or cultural critique, and that is to simply let oneself be pained, and perhaps deepened, by her story. Instead of theorizing, I would rather let my heart break. An

Emily Dickinson poem I keep thinking of in relation to Pat's life may serve to describe her better than psychologizing or philosophizing can. I've changed the gender in the original from male to female.

Lay this laurel on the one
Too intrinsic for renown.
Laurel, veil your deathless tree—
Her you chasten—that is she.

As for Vidia, my inclination is the same. Nothing could be easier than to condemn him for the way he treated Pat, Margaret, Paul Theroux, Anthony Powell, and countless other people. But to condemn him serves no purpose other than perhaps to make oneself feel better by comparison. French knew what he was doing when he chose for the title of his book the phrase—a phrase of Naipaul's—"the world is what it is." A plain acknowledgment of terrible facts is better than expostulations full of self-righteousness and blame. My guess is that the degree of misery Vidia experienced in his life can hardly be calculated. In the second section of *Enigma,* he talks about having a recurring dream in which his head is about to explode. My guess is that this is the tip of the iceberg. As French notes more than once, Vidia was not introspective; his perceptiveness was directed outward toward others. The Buddhist teacher Pema Chödrön writes: "The most fundamental aggression to ourselves, the most fundamental harm we can do ourselves, is to remain ignorant by not having the courage and the respect to look at ourselves honestly and gently." Perhaps the defensive posture Naipaul adopted toward the world as a boy, the posture of contempt described in *A House for Mr. Biswas,* which became his signature both in private and in public, prevented him from looking honestly at himself, since it would have shattered the image of superiority he'd cultivated for so long, an image he needed desperately, one that was rhetorical and strategic as well as self-protective.

Around the time he announced to Pat that he intended to move into Dairy Cottage without her, Vidia wrote in a rare moment of self-reflection: "What is the truth about my situation at the age of 51? After the life of the writer, the labour entailed by the vocation, I am still as dissatisfied . . . as empty as at the beginning." Whatever the case may be as far as Vidia's suffering is concerned, my wish is that he may venture further along the path he began to make for himself in *The Enigma of Arrival,* a path beginning to bend inward, slowly curving away from observation of the world around him, allowing him to approach the world within, a path that may one day take him to the threshold of his heart.

The whole time I'd been writing about Vidia and Pat, comparing myself to Pat, I had of course been comparing my husband to Vidia; there were parallels, and for a while this disturbed me. My husband, I knew, was not at all like Vidia in the ways that mattered most, but I was obsessed by the similarities. Then one day, the fog cleared. I remembered a time when we were living in Chicago and I was scheduled to speak at a conference in Milwaukee. I'd decided to go by train. We knew where the train station was but had never been there. I'd been planning to take a taxi when, on the morning of the conference, at the last minute, my husband offered to drive me to the station. I was little unsure about it, but accepted. It took us a while to find the street the station was on, and then to negotiate the one-way traffic. Time was short. There was no place to park; we had to drive past the station and turn a corner before he could pull up. I flew out of the car, got my bags from the trunk, waved good-bye, and took off. I ran around the corner and down the block, entered the enormous building and found my way to the ticket counter, then searched frantically through the huge, cavernous spaces for signs leading to the track my train was on. Still running with my briefcase and overnight bag, I made my way through dark passages to the even darker platform, mounted the high steps of the venerable train carriage, and struggled through the dimly lit car to a seat. I was in the process of stowing my luggage when I happened to look out the window and there was my husband, a small man in a giant parka looking like a gnome, standing on the platform, peering through the window at me with an expression of great concern on his face. Somehow, he had managed to park the car, run to the station, find the ticket window, locate the right platform, and get there in time to make sure *I* had gotten there. I'll never forget that moment. It summed up his lifetime of concern for me. Not just feelings of concern, but actions taken. If I had ever doubted it, I knew then that this man loved me as much as was humanly possible. Like Ann Patchett arriving at the Mayo Clinic in time for her husband's surgery, my husband had gotten me to Union Station and then made sure that I was on the train.

17

Reading through the Night

What is the best way to live with a chronic illness? Do you keep
hope alive by seeking new treatments, visiting new doctors, and
keeping up with the latest research? (This is exhausting.) Or do
you accept your condition, surrender to the situation, and learn
to live as you are? I hobble back and forth between the two possibilities. For periods of time, I try whatever new treatment options
arise—some work somewhat for a while and then cease to make
a difference; and for longer periods I accept my condition as best
I can, checking occasionally to see if anything new has emerged
on the medical front. And since, so far, nothing has, at least as
far as treatment is concerned, the question then becomes, how do
you live life at half-mast? For people with my condition, though
I can make suggestions for what to try and give hints on dodging
certain bullets, when it comes right down to it, I don't have solid
answers. All I have to go on is my own experience, which is vari-
able and often difficult.

The cycle of relapse and recovery dominates my life and, I suspect, the lives of many people with ME/cfs. I go from a normal
level of tiredness and the usual symptoms to a period when everything intensifies and I slip down the slope from a viable existence
into a phase where, no matter how much I rest, I have no energy
and know I'm not going to feel better any time soon. The old
formulas are useless; reading is only of minimal assistance. Even
the things I fall back on when my health has gone downhill, like

taking a warm bath, don't work. There's nothing to look forward to except, in Dickinson's phrase, "miles on miles of naught." I lie there, sick, sometimes angry, sometimes sorry for myself, thinking my thoughts, and, as a spiritual teacher I once had told us: "Your thoughts are not your friends." This is the darkest part of the night.

Depression and despair are the twin enemies. Once either of them sets in, I can no longer summon the will or the concentration to do the few things that have a chance of helping at times like this. Over the many years I've had this illness, antidepressants have occasionally kept me from pitching over the cliffs of fall I dread the most. But when the danger passes, I stop the medication because I don't want to be cut off from my experience, whatever it is, if I can possibly help it.

In many ways having chronic fatigue syndrome is like being very old. Staying with my mother in her apartment when she was in her nineties and I was in my sixties, I noticed we had about the same energy level. The similarity goes further. As you age you lose many of the capacities you used to have—the capacity to hear, to see, to move about the world at will, to have an idea that you can then carry out—and this, shall we say, makes it hard to maintain a positive attitude. It's the same with ME. One's ability to do things is sharply diminished; the inner life becomes paramount. When the body fails, unless you've developed other resources, you're in for it. If I hadn't learned to meditate some years ago and developed a spiritual life, I don't know how I would have survived.

So when the dark night descends, and I can no longer do anything very much, what do I do? I firm up my meditation practice, read spiritual books in small doses, take short walks in nature, and pray. When I have any energy at all, I see friends. This is only a pared-down version of what I do in normal circumstances, but it's all I know. I save up energy by going nowhere and doing nothing for days on end, and then splurge it on something I know will raise my spirits—nothing fancy—no skydiving or foreign travel—but something simple like going to the movies with my husband. When I'm feeling terrible, I call friends and complain, knowing they will be sympathetic. If I can cry, that helps. So does getting angry, railing at God or whatever force has visited this fate on me. I used to have fits of rage at regular intervals, and they seemed to clear the air and give me energy for a while. But though I still resist the illness when times are bad, I don't want to attack it anymore; it's taught me too much. As one chronic fatigue sufferer told me, the thing is to see the illness as part of your life, to integrate it, understand it as an element of growth. So I try to expand around the feelings of impotence and despair, make room for them, let them come and go as somewhat unwelcome guests until I can live with them without panicking. Not focusing on what I haven't got but on what's close at hand. My cat is a great solace in the dark times, and petting other people's dogs. It's a time when no one thing helps. Something can, but you have to let it reveal itself.

Reading has to be rationed. If depression has started to set in, mentally occupying a substitute world gives the negative emotions that are roiling inside a chance to increase in strength. Depression deepens, and the basement is suddenly several stories further down than you remembered. When things have gotten very bad, moment-to-moment attention is the only thing possible. Despite what some self-help books say, strong affirmations like "I am healed" don't work for me, since I lack the conviction needed to support them and they make me feel ridiculous and ashamed. But over the years I've found there are things I can say that, with luck, will alter my mood by the hairsbreadth needed to turn it in the right direction. These are very simple statements like "This won't last forever; it never has" or "Just relax, and go with it." Statements like these keep me from making the way I'm feeling at the moment into such a big deal; they remind me that it will pass and isn't the end of the world. And they get me off the hook of having to accomplish anything. It used to be that if I couldn't do anything productive, not even read, I'd say to myself, well, I'll just clean out this drawer, hoping it would make me feel better. But it never did. Now I say, let's see how little you can do. The challenge of having absolutely no expectations of myself comes as a welcome relief. It allows me, at least sometimes, to see resting as a pleasure and a luxury, rather than as a weight I have to carry.

These are my strategies when health and the hope of recovery die and I can see nothing but illness ahead. There's no formula. Just inching forward intuitively from minute to minute, hour to hour, listening to what experience has taught—you can relax, it won't last forever—and then watching things unfold. That way, if good feelings break in unexpectedly, I'm there to receive them, just as I'm there to feel the misery. All of which is by way of saying that reading, though a salve to the mind and a balm to the spirit, cannot bridge the deepest chasms of experience. These must be crossed without the aid of books. You can read through much of the night, but not all of it.

Day to day, though, reading is my rod and my staff. When I'm neither on an upswing or a down, but picking my way along trying to avoid a relapse, I need reading to keep my mind busy while my body rests. When putting myself together in the morning wears me out and I need to lie down until the well of energy fills again, I read. When I've gone to the drugstore to refill a prescription and bought a few groceries and need to recover from the exertion, I read. When I've emptied the dishwasher and put the laundry away and have to stop and rest, I read. When I've watered the plants and changed the kitty litter and have to pause before I do any more, I read. Several times a day I stretch out on my bed or the sofa, with a book propped on my chest, and enter the stream of experience another person has created. There's pleasure in this moment, even a feeling of luxury, as I let myself go into the alternate universe of a book. But I haven't always appreciated the opportunity.

I've spent a lot of time resenting having to read so much, seen it as a placeholder, a necessary but pernicious substitute for life. Why can't I be like other people and get to do something else for a change, run an errand, go shopping, play tennis? Lifting my head from a book, I've looked into space and felt a wave of despair sweep through me. Is this it? I wonder, will there ever be anything more than this? And then I remind myself that in a few hours or a few days or a few weeks, I'll be well enough to do something, and let the moment pass. My illness is the perfect prescription for my recurrent sense, established long ago, that I'm getting a raw deal, being shortchanged, having it harder than other people. Seeing through this is what I have to learn over and over again.

In my teens I read a science fiction story about a race of exceptional men who rebelled against the domination of a galactic imperial force. When captured, they received a punishment worse than any I have heard of since. Each one was encased in cement and suspended, upside down, in the ocean of some distant planet. Although they could communicate telepathically with others of their race, they were unable to see, hear, speak, move—or die. Their immobility and isolation—conscious and everlasting— terrified me. Over the years I've spent stretched out on beds and sofas, reading my life away, pitying myself because all I could do *was* read, it never occurred to me to imagine what it would have been like to do without it. Life as I'd known it was over, but at least I wasn't suspended upside down in cement on an ocean floor at the far end of the galaxy! Unlike the rebel telepaths, I had a way out: I could read. And not only that. After several years, I could write, too, which allowed me the luxury of sustained effort. When you're ill and options are limited, an ongoing project is a gift from the gods because it allows you to dedicate yourself to the accomplishment of something and watch it grow as a result of your efforts. What a privilege that is. Illness is isolating and frustrating because it cuts you off from a wide range of experience. But the worst part is the debilitating effect of not having meaningful work to do. Writing, when I was finally able to do it, lifted me out of self-pity as nothing else could.

Being ill a long time has taught me that having a focus for one's life is almost as much a necessity as food and water. Simply taking care of oneself is not enough, at least it hasn't been for me. When I began to be able to write again, and started this book, my life changed. Writing provided my day with a center of gravity, brought my faculties to bear on a task I knew how to do that gave me pleasure and satisfaction. Like reading, I enjoyed it more than I ever had when I did it for a living. It was as if someone had thrown me a life preserver and said, here, grab hold of this, it will rescue you from uselessness. Hold on.

But as I began to feel happy I also began to feel guilty. (Some people can feel guilty about anything.) The guilt stemmed from no longer having to experience the pain of confronting life without a goal. In Florida I'd staved off depression by working on the garden with my landscaper, and in the Catskills by learning to paint in watercolors, but underneath I was still adrift. Now, writing had given me a reprieve from that emptiness: it provided a kind of existential anchor that those occupations had not and kept me from having to wrestle with the conviction that my life had no purpose, made no difference, and was out of contact with practically everything. Writing took away the feeling that I was floating in a permanent limbo halfway between life and death where nothing would ever happen.

But does life have to have a purpose? I'd spent enough time wondering about this, as I whiled away the hours doing puzzles and playing games of solitaire, to need an answer to this question, and to know that there is more than one. Rabbi Abraham Heschel's saying, "just to be is a blessing; just to live is holy," represents the view that it's absurd to expect life to conform itself to this or that end. Such a demand misses the essence of life, which is being itself, an approach not popular in American culture where books with titles like *The Purpose-Driven Life* are hugely successful. The committed life, the life devoted to a cause or to the attainment of a goal, is what most Americans, myself included, understand: Eleanor Roosevelt, Mahatma Gandhi, Mother Teresa, Martin Luther King. But without disputing the value of a life of service — whose joys and rewards I'd experienced both in my job and in volunteer work — my meditation practice leads me to believe that Rabbi Heschel's view is correct. A sentence from R. H. Blythe's *Zen in English Literature and Oriental Classics,* which I read when I was nineteen, still echoes in my head: "Awaken the mind without fixing it anywhere." A state of openness and receptivity probably brings us closer to life than following a mind-generated plan. My own experience convinces me that there's a level of being beyond the mind and the emotions, where goals and aims dissolve and one's very self loses its boundaries. Nevertheless I'm here to testify that to live without purpose, without goals, is terribly difficult. Your hands lie empty. Body and mind are restless and unsatisfied. There's nothing to reinforce the ego. The spirit longs for a state of devotedness to something. You feel you might as well die.

Do I want to be like Kurt Wallander, for whom a job supplies the role of life purpose and who almost never looks over his shoulder to catch a glimpse of something else? Not really. I've been that route and know it's just a stage along the way. It's when you look up from your task — not when you're concentrating on it — that the world reveals itself. But still, I know I'm not so deeply connected to the source of being that when goals are taken away I can face with equanimity the night of emptiness and uselessness. If I were so connected, the question of having goals wouldn't arise. For now, despite the guilty twinges, I'm unspeakably grateful for the reprieve writing has given me and bless the day I received *Sir Vidia's Shadow,* which brought me friendship and work to do all at the same time.

I can write only for short periods. I have to pace myself. If I'm not careful, I'll use up too much energy and have to pay the price. So when I feel momentum slowing and energy fading away, what do I do? I read, of course. Writing is the existential life preserver, but reading is the ballast, the cushion, the absorber of shocks, the tranquilizer, the recharging device, the inspiration, and the energizer. Reading is my patent medicine: it grows hair, eases cramps, settles the digestion, lowers the heart rate, and helps me fall asleep.

In Florida one spring when my energy was extremely low, I'd tried, to no avail, all the remedies my doctors had prescribed. I took medicine for immune support and shoveled supplements down my throat. My vegetables were all organic. I avoided sugar, gluten, and caffeine, and took alcohol, if at all, in the most modest doses. I kept regular sleeping hours when the insomnia that goes with the disease let me and was careful not to exert myself too much. But to no avail. I had to cancel the few appointments on my almost empty calendar and knew I was headed for depression if I didn't do something soon. Then one day on TV I heard about a book called *The China Study* by Colin Campbell, a top researcher in nutrition at Cornell who had discovered that populations who ate a diet containing little or no meat or dairy products almost never died from the two diseases that kill most people in the United States, heart disease and cancer. I bought the book and read it, and it was so well-argued and intelligent that it convinced me a vegan diet was the best possible for human health and ought to raise my energy level. There was nothing to lose. I found vegan recipes on the Internet which made me feel resourceful and creative, sat in my garden at lunchtime under the lancewood tree and, as I watched the monarchs sip nectar from the flowers, munched happily on king-size salads tossed in tahini dressing. Within two weeks I'd lost ten pounds. My bowels functioned like magic. My figure looked good. But after a few weeks more I had, if anything, less energy than when I started. Instead of growing strong, I grew weaker, and then weaker still. The diet was not for me.

Verging on despair—having returned, sparingly, to more traditional sources of protein—and casting about for something to take up the slack—I needed to feel better psychologically, if not physically—I remembered the way my cousin Richard, a philosophy professor at Agnes Scott College, had once talked about the novels of Anthony Trollope, recalling the happiness in his voice as he described how good he felt in the world Trollope had created. Not long before, I'd read one of his novels and liked it. I decided to put my money on Trollope. For a dollar and change I downloaded onto my Kindle the five chronicles of Barsetshire and the six Palliser chronicles, lay down on the seagrass sofa, clicked to page one of *The Warden,* and began.

Day after day, week after week, the novels carried me through the long afternoons of languor and inanition. The sun grew stronger as it came in through the Venetian blinds, striping the wicker rocking chairs and the plum-colored Chinese rug with its wide indigo border. As I lay there, I luxuriated in the knowledge that there was practically no end to this enjoyment. Clicking from page to page, I let the afternoon hours unreel, and still there were more pages to enjoy, more books waiting to be devoured. Cushioned by the troubles of bishops and curates, and the intrigues of countesses and ministers of state, I was protected from my own troubles. Walking the grounds of *The Small House at Allington,* I was safe. Slowly and mysteriously the wellsprings of my energy began to fill. Aided as well by the discovery of vitamin and mineral infusions, administered intravenously, against the advice of my expert doctor, my strength returned to the point where I could get on a plane and go north again. I had won that battle, for the time being.

I will not forget the gratitude I felt as I lay there in the sun on that sofa, when from time to time, my dear cat, Teddy, would climb onto my chest and keep me company—gratitude that these novels had been written and that I was lucky enough to be able to read them. For once I wasn't worried that I was making no contribution to society; I didn't bother to feel guilty that I wasn't meditating or listening to music. I was too caught up in the fortunes of struggling clerics, proud aristocrats, and young, unmarried women in search of husbands. These characters needed me to care about their vicissitudes and to fret over their destinies. It was happy employment. It even made me feel useful.

Reader, if you are about to have an operation requiring several weeks of convalescence, or are recovering from a disastrous love affair, or planning to go on a very long trip, trust me: Trollope is your man. Once you fall under his spell, he can get you through some very rough territory. Trollope is the ideal long-term escape; he won't let you down.

So there it is, the e-word, escape, the thing I've been accusing myself of continually for the last ten years. Reading as drug, as addiction, as hiding place, as coward's way out, as protection from misery, ignoble time-killer. Poe knew about this. He wrote in "The Raven": "'Wretch,' I cried, 'thy God hath lent thee—by his angels he has sent thee / Respite—respite and nepenthe.'" Nepenthe, you may remember, is a potion that induces forgetfulness of pain and sorrow. Poe used alcohol as his nepenthe. He must have needed it. I use reading. Over and over, I've accused myself of laziness, fecklessness, spinelessness, good-for-nothingness as I lay on a bed or a sofa and consumed some novel. I'd ask other people what they thought: was all this reading a bad thing? Did they think I should be doing something else to fill my days while my body acquired the energy to be active? But no one condemned me. A friend who also has ME said the wisest thing: reading's all right as long as you don't use it to cover up emotional problems. By and large, I didn't use reading that way. I had learned, as I've said, that covering misery over with reading only makes it worse.

Castigating myself for too much reading stems from my old habit of self-criticism, of course. Who else, stricken with a debilitating chronic disease, would criticize herself for too much reading? Now, when I start to berate myself for being a slacker as I ease down onto the sofa with a book in my hand, I consciously change gears and allow myself to enjoy resting. I'm in recovery from the notion that reading is bad if it's used to calm nerves, relax the body, and distract the mind from obsessive thinking. When you're sick and there's not much else you can do, depriving yourself of its solace is a little like not putting on a warm coat when it's cold outside. People with common sense arrive at this conclusion right away. It's taken me somewhat longer. As part of the process, my struggles with guilt have made me think about what, in the context of reading, "escape" really means.

Is resting when you're tired a form of escape? Is it avoidance to take your mind off problems that can't be resolved by worrying about them? Is innocent pleasure that's there for the taking to be resisted on principle? A humble acceptance of the enjoyments the world has to offer is better than a proud refusal to be lured by their sweetness. One of the hardest things in life to learn is compassion for one's own needs and limitations. Wanting to be more than we are, which is to say, without weakness, flaws, or mistakes in judgment, we create further difficulties. In short, I've finally accepted that reading is a blessing I've been lucky enough to be able to receive.

When we enter a text as refuge, it needs to take us away from whatever form of bad weather is beating us down at the moment. It needs to gather us into a world where we feel not only protected but nourished; it must become a second womb. What's wanted is to go into this other world and not come out for a long time, to stay there, and be born again. By whatever chemistry or magic, the words of the text re-form, rejoin, and realign the pieces of the shattered self, according to patterns more congenial and enlivening. Lucky the man who finds a book that can take away his misery, soothe his agitated spirit, and bring it a marvelous dream. Lucky the woman who happens upon a book as good as a nurse or a fairy godmother that takes away her pain and finds her a dress for the ball.

Where reading is concerned it's good to be your own doctor. Learn to self-medicate. Don't take your friend's word for it that a book is good, or a reviewer's. Don't be persuaded by the title or the cover art. Try the book out, taste it first, read the opening pages before you commit. And, once inside, don't feel obliged to continue just because you started. I'm still learning to let go of the notion that I'm a quitter if I don't read every book I start to the last page. If a book makes you feel bad consistently, put it aside. Life is too short to squander on books that bring you down. But by this I don't mean one should avoid unpleasantness.

One more thing. Reading for pleasure is good. But if I've learned anything on this journey, it's that when a book upsets or troubles you, you need to find out why. It's a signal that something important is going on and it's worth taking the time to investigate. When a sentence or a scene or a character grabs your attention and won't let go, you can be sure it's the symptom of some inner business unresolved. This is your chance. Instead of letting the experience fade, ask yourself why you feel that way, ask what it is about the incident that could have produced this reaction—in you—and if nothing occurs, keep on asking. Eventually the answer will come, sometimes in the form of a memory that seems unrelated to the matter in question, but don't be fooled. The unconscious doesn't make mistakes. If you stick with the process, the ghost will rise from the text and deliver its message. And should you discover something you'd rather not know, all the better. Such knowledge is precious and leads to healing. It took me two years to find out why I was so enthralled by *Sir Vidia's Shadow,* and I'm glad I did: two years is not long. Books that captivate without stirring up any unwanted thoughts or emotions are wonderful; books that shine a light into dark places are like gold. They come along less often than the other kind, but when they do, the opportunity is tremendous. See where the trouble leads. You have no idea what painful knot might come undone. The thing is not to be afraid.

Afterword

Readers may remember my struggles to forgive Theroux for the way he treats women in his writing. In several chapters of *My Other Life* he characterizes them as sexual predators and himself as their innocent victim, behavior that didn't square with the kind of person Theroux seemed otherwise to be—a man who loved his wife and children, worked devotedly at his craft, and took care of his responsibilities—a man I liked. To explain his behavior toward women, my friend Maggie and I, as we sat among the sparrows at the Côté France, had theorized that Theroux must have been traumatized by a woman early in life, probably his mother—there was no way around it—and, no way to know. But there is now.

A year after this manuscript was completed, Theroux published a partially fictionalized but devastating portrait of his mother and family of origin in a five-hundred-page novel called *Mother Land*. Though in an interview with WBUR in Boston, Theroux says 60 percent is true and 40 percent is fiction, the impulses behind the book seem 100 percent autobiographical. It appears that Maggie and I had been right. *Mother Land* is the furious, vehement, nearly out-of-control indictment of a diabolically cruel and powerful mother. Considering the way his mother treated him—indifference, rejection, and outright malice were what he got, assuming this account is not far from the truth—it's remarkable that Theroux turned out to be the decent, intelligent, and productive human being he comes through as in his work, and small wonder that he harbored a deep resentment against women that could spring to life at any moment. If ever there was an explanation for misogyny, this was it.

I read *Mother Land* in a hurry—the way it asks to be read. The novel feels as if the author couldn't stop himself from writing it, or write it fast enough. After decades of being stored away, scene after scene of childhood humiliation and defeat come tumbling out, filled with an anger and shame as hot as they were on the day the event that caused them first occurred. One of the cruelest incidents takes place in adulthood, when his older brother writes a scathing review of Theroux's latest novel, replete with personal attacks. This was the brother Theroux had had a special relationship with growing up, and he's devastated. On top of that, his mother pretends to know nothing about it—and when she's told, doesn't care. All seven children were victimized by their mother in various ways and as adults still vie constantly for her approval, waging poisonous, byzantine struggles among themselves, while she, the queen bee, the empress on her throne, covertly eggs them on.

Since gossip was oxygen for Mother, she asked me in the canniest way what I had heard, pretending not to know anything so as to compare my version of a story with the one she had already been told, always hungry for the smallest detail of frailty or frittering away money. Her eyes glittered with pleasure at a choice tidbit, and hearing something truly disgraceful, she could not prevent herself from laughing out loud, showing her yellow teeth to their wolfish roots.

In the interview, Theroux says that in the novel his mother is made out to be much worse than she was; be that as it may, the glittering eyes, the laugh, and the yellow teeth with their wolfish roots suggest that Theroux is ridding himself of demons; one feels the force of pent-up feelings looking for an outlet—the goal, a release from pain, with a side of revenge. There's also a quantum of pleasure involved. I sensed Theroux's satisfaction at finally being able to reach the marrow of his suffering and relished the agility and expressivity of his prose, energized by the need to bear witness to past and present wrongs. Sometimes, as I read, the accounts of treachery and betrayal took their toll and the toxicity outweighed the virtuosity. I didn't want to have to feel, again and again, the pain of the wounds he'd sustained. But mostly, I gobbled it up.

Theroux had used writing before as a way to deal with disturbing events—the break with Naipaul, his divorce—and it produced some of his best work. This time he takes on the biggest challenge of all, his traumatic childhood, and gives it everything he's got. To see the book as a success—which I do—one has to accept that Theroux has not reached the stage of wanting to make peace with his past. He isn't ready. He doesn't try that hard to discover what made his mother the way she was, and though sometimes he describes his brothers and sisters with great sympathy as they suffer at each other's hands, often he doesn't show them much compassion. He can't. He has to get everything off his chest, testify to hurts received but never understood, to wrongs whose perpetrators were never called to account. He needs to destroy the myth that he had belonged to a large, happy family with an exemplary mother before he can begin to heal.

But *Mother Land* isn't just Theroux's chance to blow off steam and get back at people who hurt him. As he relives the events he relates, Theroux comes to new realizations about himself as a writer and a human being. With its brilliant portrayals of bad family scenarios, *Mother Land* showed me that the effort to deal with one's past can be effective without complete understanding and forgiveness. In fact, seeing through a glass darkly is the very nature of the enterprise. One does the best one can. In *Mother Land* Theroux explains patterns of behavior that recur throughout his work, such as his penchant for secrecy, reliance on deceit, and reluctance to confront authority—strategies forged in the furnace of his upbringing. Most of all, the book evokes sympathy, not just for the sufferings of childhood but also for the effects that his childhood had on Theroux's later life. Who knew that the man who left his wife and children repeatedly to get on trains to far-off places did so, not just in order to write books, but because he was still trying to escape from his hellish family of origin? Written with skills acquired over a lifetime and with the passion of a person still seeking his salvation, *Mother Land* provides evidence that growth in self-understanding can be achieved at a late stage of life—Theroux is in his seventies—evidence that the story is not over yet and that new insight and change can take place until the end.

ACKNOWLEDGMENTS

First I want to thank Sharon Anson ("Maggie" in the text) for giving me *Sir Vidia's Shadow* and for believing in this project from first to last. Her devotion and enthusiasm kept me afloat and helped me believe in myself—not to mention her line editing of every single page. Next, my gratitude goes to Catherine Michelle Adams, inspired developmental editor, brilliant reader, and eloquent responder. Her intuitive grasp of what I was aiming for was uncanny; I could not have done it without her guidance and support.

Several people read the entire manuscript and gave me precious feedback: Mary Beth Rose, Peninah Petruck, Peter Fulton, Arlene Metrick, Philip Davis, and Stanley Fish. I can't say how grateful I am for their advice, their support, and their attention. Marianna Torgovnick, Rima Walker, Myra Jehlen, and Janet Malcolm read one or more chapters and responded with great insight. Thank you, friends. I'm grateful to Lindsay Waters for his positive feedback and to Melissa Flashman, my agent, for the same.

To my editor at the University of Virginia Press, Eric Brandt, thanks for being responsive and helpful, I so appreciate it. Thanks to Susan Murray, copy editor, for being such a pleasure to work with, and to Ellen Satrom, managing editor, for her kindness and attentiveness. One is in good hands at Virginia.

☾

Finally, on a more personal note, thank you, Bobbi Newman, for your insight into my marriage and my self. Thank you, Patty Whitehouse, for saying the words that lit up the landscape of my life—you know what they are. And to my dear Stan, who had the humility and largeness of heart to let me write about him and our relationship and not mind—I love you so.

WORKS CITED

Athill, Diana. *Somewhere towards the End: A Memoir*. New York: W. W. Norton, 2009.

Blythe, R. H. *Zen in English Literature and Oriental Classics*. Tokyo: Hokuseido Press, 1942.

Burnett, Frances Hodgson. *The Secret Garden*. London: William Heinemann, 1911.

Campbell, T. Colin, and Thomas M. Campbell II. *The China Study: The Most Comprehensive Study of Nutrition Ever Conducted and the Startling Implications for Diet, Weight Loss, and Long-term Health*. Dallas: BenBella, 2005.

de Botton, Alain. *The Art of Travel*. New York: Pantheon, 2002.

D'Erasmo, Stacey. *The Art of Intimacy: The Space Between*. Minneapolis: Graywolf, 2013.

Dogen. *The Essential Dogen: Writings of the Great Zen Master*. Edited by Kazuaki Tanahashi and Peter Levitt. Boston: Shambhala, 2013.

Ferrante, Elena. *The Days of Abandonment*. Translated by Ann Goldstein. New York: Europa, 2005.

Freire, Paulo. *Pedagogy of the Oppressed*. Translated by Myra Bergman Ramos. New York: Herder and Herder, 1970.

French, Patrick. *The World Is What It Is: The Authorized Biography of V. S. Naipaul*. New York: Alfred A. Knopf, 2008.

Gornick, Vivian. *Fierce Attachments: A Memoir*. New York: Farrar Straus and Giroux, 1987.

Hawthorne, Nathaniel. *The Scarlet Letter*. Boston: Ticknor, Reed, and Fields, 1850.

Hemingway, Ernest. *In Our Time*. New York: Boni and Liveright, 1925.

Huysmans, J. K. *À rebours*. Paris: G. Charpentier, 1884.

Jones, Alden. *The Blind Masseuse: A Traveler's Memoir from Costa Rica to Cambodia*. Madison: University of Wisconsin Press, 2013.

Klinkenberg, Jeff. *Alligators in B-Flat: Improbable Tales from the Files of Real Florida*. Gainesville: University Press of Florida, 2013.

Krauss, Nicole. *The History of Love*. New York: W. W. Norton, 2005.

Mankell, Henning. *An Event in Autumn*. Translated by Laurie Thompson. New York: Vintage, 2014.

———. *The Man Who Smiled*. Translated by Laurie Thompson. New York: New Press, 2006.

———. *One Step Behind*. Translated by Ebba Segerberg. New York: New Press, 2002.

———. *The White Lioness*. Translated by Laurie Thompson. New York: New Press, 1998.

Mayle, Peter. *A Year in Provence*. New York: Alfred A. Knopf, 1990.

Naipaul, V. S. *A Bend in the River*. New York: Alfred A. Knopf, 1979.

———. *Between Father and Son: Family Letters*. New York: Alfred A. Knopf, 2000.

———. *The Enigma of Arrival*. New York: Alfred A. Knopf, 1987.

———. *A House for Mr. Biswas*. New York: Alfred A. Knopf, 1961.

———. *In a Free State*. New York: Alfred A. Knopf, 1971.

———. *Miguel Street*. New York: Vanguard, 1959.

———. *The Writer and the World: Essays*. New York: Alfred A. Knopf, 2002.

Osorio, Rufino. *A Gardener's Guide to Florida's Native Plants*. Gainesville: University Press of Florida, 2001.

Palmer, Parker J. *Let Your Life Speak: Listening for the Voice of Vocation*. San Francisco: Jossey-Bass, 1999.

Patchett, Ann. *Bel Canto*. New York: HarperCollins, 2001.

———. *This Is the Story of a Happy Marriage*. New York: HarperCollins, 2013.

Pirsig, Robert M. *Zen and the Art of Motorcycle Maintenance: An Inquiry into Values*. New York: William Morrow, 1974.

Proust, Marcel. *In Search of Lost Time*. Translated by C. K. Scott Moncrieff and Terence Kilmartin. New York: Modern Library, 2003.

Remen, Rachel Naomi. *My Grandfather's Blessings: Stories of Strength, Refuge, and Belonging*. New York: Penguin, 2000.

Sacks, Oliver. *The Man Who Mistook His Wife for a Hat and Other Clinical Tales*. New York: Summit, 1985.

Stein, Sara. *Noah's Garden: Restoring the Ecology of Our Own Back Yards*. New York: Houghton Mifflin, 1993.

Stewart, Rory. *The Places in Between*. New York: Harcourt, 2006.

Suzuki, Shunryu. *Zen Mind, Beginner's Mind: Informal Talks on Zen Meditation and Practice.* Boston: Shambhala, 2006.

Theroux, Paul. *The Great Railway Bazaar: By Train through Asia.* Boston: Houghton Mifflin, 1975.

——. *Mother Land.* Boston: Houghton Mifflin, 2017.

——. *My Other Life.* Boston: Houghton Mifflin, 1996.

——. *My Secret History.* New York: G. P. Putnam's Sons, 1989.

——. *The Old Patagonian Express: By Train through the Americas.* Boston: Houghton Mifflin, 1979.

——. *Sir Vidia's Shadow: A Friendship across Five Continents.* Boston: Houghton Mifflin, 1998.

Tompkins, Jane. *A Life in School: What the Teacher Learned.* Cambridge, MA: Perseus, 1996.

Trollope, Anthony. *The Small House at Allington.* London: George Smith, 1864.

——. *The Warden.* London: Longman, 1855.

Wright, Richard. *Black Boy.* New York: Harper, 1945.